$$$ HOW TO $$$
SELL &
RE-SELL
YOUR WRITING

$$$ HOW TO $$$
SELL &
RE-SELL
YOUR WRITING

Duane Newcomb

Cincinnati, Ohio

92 91 90 89 88 87   5 4 3 2 1

Library of Congress Cataloging-in-Publication Data

Newcomb, Duane G.
  How to sell & re-sell your writing.

  Bibliography: p.
  Includes index.
  1. Authorship—Handbooks, manuals, etc.
I. Title.   II. Title: How to sell and re-sell your writing.
PN147.N47   1987   808'.02   87-29568
ISBN 0-89879-296-7

Design by Judy Allan.

Acknowledgments

I want to thank my many students who helped me turn the classroom into an article laboratory. To Bud Gardner of American River College, Sacramento, who has combined some of my methods with his own unique talents and taken them much farther than I thought possible. Also my appreciation to Frank Zdy who taught me much about the science and art of selling everything you write.

Thanks, too, to my agent Jane Jordan Browne for making this book possible in the first place. Most of all I must express my gratitude to my wife Karen who helps me, in a thousand ways, with every writing project.

Contents

Introduction

When I first started teaching writing, I ran into a paradox. Many of my students who could write well never sold a single article. Yet students whose writing wasn't as good sold articles repeatedly.

One lady had taken my class twice. The third time she was enrolled she came to me and said, "I'm going to sell an article this semester if it's the last thing I do!" I thought, Lady, it will be the last thing. This person, as far as I was concerned, was one of the world's worst writers. Her sentences rambled so much that I had trouble following her chain of thought through a manuscript.

The woman and her husband had just closed in a passageway between their kitchen and garage. She wrote an article on this remodeling project and mailed it to *Handyman*. Within four weeks she received a check for two hundred dollars. Next she queried *California Home* to see if they would like a piece about the remodeling of a living room. They not only wanted the article, they sent a photographer to take pictures. The woman also mailed *Mechanic's Illustrated* (now renamed *Home Mechanix*) a manuscript about the backyard barbecue she and her husband were building. This brought another $150. The last time I heard about her, she had sold almost a hundred articles and was working on a book called *Simple Backyard Projects*.

This opened my eyes. I had long known that an article must be specifically targeted to a magazine's needs, but I hadn't realized just how important that was. Every article the woman submitted had been poorly written, but each piece was exactly what that particular magazine needed.

This incident and a number of other similar cases caused me to formulate what I call "Newcomb's Rules One and Two." Newcomb's Rule Number One says: Anyone who can write a clear sentence can learn to write salable articles.

Newcomb's Second Rule states: Every article must be targeted directly to the magazine you want to hit.

My next problem was to translate all of this into some sort of system beginning writers could use to help them break into print and that more advanced writers could put to work to help them increase their article sales.

The result was what my classes laughingly called "The Newcomb Method." And that's what this book is all about. The first part helps you understand writing from the magazine's point of view. It also gives you a way to find a number of markets for an idea or to start with a particular magazine and create a number of ideas tailored to that magazine.

The remainder of the book covers establishing yourself with an editor, turning out writing in volume, hitting the major magazines, selling the same article over and over, and using your files to produce even more articles and sales.

Does the system work? You bet it does. Not only have I sold several thousand articles and a number of books myself, but my students have done far better than I ever expected. A number of beginners sold their first articles and went on to place the next thirty or forty without a rejection. Many have become contributors to the major magazines. And a few have received book advances of $100,000 or more. Altogether they have now sold over a million and a half dollars worth of articles and books.

What they have done, you too can do. Selling to magazines is easy. It simply takes a clear understanding of how to go about it. This book is intended to be a guide to help you on your way. I suggest you read through it quickly the first time, then come back and pick up what seems especially important to you. Finally, try out some of the ideas with your own writing.

Above all, keep at it. Writing, like other professions, has its ups and downs. But I have learned from experience that if you are determined to make it, you will. With a little effort, you too can join the ranks of the selling writers and go on to make a number of sales to many magazines.

May you have a wonderful time and much good luck on your journey.

Duane Newcomb

1. Acquiring Magazine Savvy

In the writing world I've discovered there are two kinds of writers. The first one comes up with an idea, puts together an article from that idea, and sends the article to a number of magazines. When the author decides that article won't sell, he or she comes up with another idea and starts the process again. Sometimes these authors sell a few articles, but it's mainly a hit-and-miss proposition. For every article they sell, they get ten or more rejections.

The second type of writer generally starts with the magazine and attempts to understand why that magazine publishes what it does. Then this writer asks, "What can I give this magazine that will meet its editorial needs?" After a period of study, this second writer begins to understand each magazine almost as well as the editor does. At this point, he or she has acquired what I call "magazine savvy."

I have had both types of writers in my classes. The first type may sell one or two articles once in a while, while writing many more. The second type often sells the first article they write and frequently go on to sell the next twenty or so without a rejection slip. Over a year's time, many of the writers who really understand the magazines may sell ninety percent of everything they write. And that's what this chapter is all about. In it I am going to give you the basics of acquiring magazine savvy. Master this and you will have tipped the scales in your favor, even before you have written one word.

UNDERSTANDING MAGAZINES AS A BUSINESS

Let's understand first what magazines are. They aren't, as some writers seem to believe, a place to show off a writer's work. Magazines are businesses in which someone has invested money in hopes of making more money in return. These businesspeople want to attract as many readers as possible so advertisers will place ads in the magazine.

The editor and publisher of a science magazine want to attract readers interested in science. Home repair magazines are supposed to attract an audience interested in fixing up their homes. Most magazines go further than this and try to reach a readership that falls within a certain age group, makes a certain amount of income, and has a particular lifestyle. This allows them to provide advertisers with a very specific target market.

THE DEMOGRAPHICS OF AN AUDIENCE

In an advertisement in *Advertising Age, Auto Week* says about its readers: "For some men, cars and motoring are one of the most important parts of their lives. They are the insiders. For them, monthly enthusiast books (magazines) are too slow. They are so involved they must have up-to-the-minute news every single week.

"These men are always the first to discover new cars, accessories, automotive-related products.

"They always know which drivers are ahead in the point standings. They are so knowledgeable, their influence is great, far out of all proportion to their number. They are the ultimate consumers, the insiders who read *Auto Week*: 99% male . . . Average age 36 . . . Average Income $69,900 . . . Own 3.7 vehicles."

Town and Country, on the other hand, says its readers "have a taste for vintage scotch. *Town and Country* readers are on their way to wealth or are already there. *Town and Country* is a special guide to our readers' special way of life."

And *Home Mechanix* reports, "Our readers have a very special point of view. They build their lives around the American Dream: home, hearth, a car or truck (or two or three). And nobody invests in it like *Home Mechanix* buyers. Spending more time and money on their homes and their cars than anything else."

All the editorial material that goes into these magazines is aimed at holding the readers they have and attracting more of the same kind. As a result, they develop a format they think will appeal to the reader they want. Every article that goes into the magazine must fit this format and help enhance the reader's perceived lifestyle.

EDITORS BUY IDEAS, NOT WRITING

This is one of the basic principles I discovered during my early writing years. I had written for a magazine called *Trailer Life* for about two years and had sold them about forty-five articles. During this time I had struck up a friendship with the editor and publisher, Art Rouse. One day at lunch I said to him, "I know you get about ninety articles a week from writers; how do you pick the ones you are going to buy?"

"As you know," Art said, "we try to buy articles that we feel our readers can use. This can encompass almost anything that has to do with trailering and recreational vehicles. The subject matter might include technical articles, travel, cooking in your trailer, trailering with the baby, single RV travel, personalities who live in trailers, full-time trailering, and a lot more.

"Every morning I look through the stack of manuscripts and read the first page. If it is an idea I can use, from my reading of that one page, I buy it. If it isn't, no matter how well it is written, I reject the article."

I asked, "What happens if you buy an article and after the first page discover it isn't very well written?"

"That's okay," Art said, "one of our editors will fix it."

WIDESPREAD PRACTICE   That was the first inkling I had that editors placed such a premium on the idea itself. Up to that time I had believed the writing was of first importance. My next eye-opener came within a few months.

I had written a query letter to *American Home** about an article titled "Do You Really Own Your Own Home?" It concerned a group of homeowners in the Napa Valley who had purchased their

*No longer published.

homes on a contract of sale. These homeowners had kept their mortgage payments current. But the firm they made the payments to hadn't passed the money on to the bank that held their mortgages. The bank was about to foreclose on the mortgages, and the homeowners stood to lose everything.

I didn't hear anything about this query for six weeks. Then at about 3 A.M. one morning, California time, I received a call from New York. Alan Borg, the building editor of *American Home,* wanted to know if I could finish the article within forty-eight hours. You bet I could.

It turned out that they needed the piece desperately for the new California edition. At this point they had only seen the query and had no idea how well I could write. But they intended to buy the article no matter what.

ANYONE CAN SUGGEST GOOD IDEAS   Another example occurred just recently. A friend of mine, freelance writer Paul Bagne, sent the magazine *Mother Jones* a query about temporary workers called "swampers." These are people hired to clean up nuclear reactors after an accident. The query he sent the editor, Mark Dowie, read:

"Tom Gear is promotions manager of the Family Bowling Lanes in North Chicago. To earn extra cash, he fixes broken-down nuclear reactors.

"He climbs into tight work spaces to plug leaky pipes. On a typical job he will absorb more radiation in a minute than most atomic power workers take in three years.

"He is part of an expanding force of temporaries hired for radioactive repairs, maintenance, and clean up. Senators, government regulators, and critics have voiced concern about this practice of spreading radiation dose and risk beyond the workplace, but most experts see the trend as a continuing, though unforeseen, cost of nuclear power.

"I can prepare for *Mother Jones* readers a 4,500-word article that investigates the use of an estimated 20,000 hired-for-exposure workers each year. By posing as an unemployed laborer, I can learn firsthand what 'jumpers' are told about risks of crawling into radioactive equipment for 'hot' repairs."

This idea brought an immediate go-ahead from Mark Dowie,

who gave Paul an assignment without seeing the article itself. He also agreed to pay for Paul to go back to Pennsylvania and join the class of workers training to be jumpers.

From all of this, I begin to realize just how important ideas are to a magazine. The problem, of course, is to figure out just what article ideas to offer particular magazines. Actually it's fairly easy. And the next several chapters will show you step-by-step exactly how to do this.

EVERY MAGAZINE HAS A FOCUS

Each magazine has a way of looking at the world (its focus) that infiltrates every article that runs in that magazine.

Popular Science says their periodical "is the magazine of what's new. Nearly every article it runs focuses on the newest and the latest."

Here are some examples of current *Popular Science* articles:

- "Fastest Bicycle in the World: 61.44 MPH." This is a new break-through bicycle that's different from the others.

- "4-Wheel Drive, 4-Wheel Steering for Future Cars." This is a brand-new development that may appear on the cars of the future.

- "The Rush to Hush Computer Printers, Say Good-bye to that Annoying Clackety-Clack with Thermal, Ink-jet and Laser Technology." This article also focuses on new developments. These advances will help solve the printer's biggest problem.

- "Hot New Tires—Racetrack Performance for Your Car." This article focuses on a new generation of tires.

Every article printed in *Popular Science* focuses on the magazine's way of looking at the world. All emphasize new developments.

The advertising for *Popular Mechanics* stresses that it is reaching for the upscale, action-oriented male market. As a result, the magazine frequently runs articles like these:

- "Television Touchdowns." The latest in the large screen televisions taps the higher income market.

- "Muscle Cars Then and Now." A look at high-powered cars is especially interesting to upscale, action-oriented males.

- "Dream Boats, High Speed on the High Seas for a Hundred Grand." This reaches for the same market.

- "Tale of the Tape: Videocamera Do's and Don'ts." This is aimed at a market that has money.

- "B-1B, Out of the Shadows: Is it a strategic weapon? Is it a flying test bed? And why have you probably never seen a photo of one?" Like the other articles, this is targeted to an action-oriented, upscale male.

All of the articles in *Popular Mechanics* are slanted to appeal to its perceived market and its way of looking at the world.

Home Mechanix says it is the magazine that "helps you manage your house and auto better." Its focus centers on helping its readers repair their homes, handle lawn and garden projects, fix up their autos, and more. As a result, it is not surprising that you find such titles as these in the magazine:

- "The Most Common House Problems and Cures." This article tells things middle-class, younger home owners can do to find and fix their problems.

- "A Kid's Country Wardrobe that Grows with Your Child." This gives details about how to make it or put it together.

- "Blankets for Weed-Free Beds." This gives instructions for making burlap blankets that insure a weed-free flower bed.

- "Workshop in your Basement." This article comes complete with how-to building instructions.

- "Season Extender for Home Gardeners." This tells about

cloches and tunnels the readers can build that allow them to grow vegetables at each end of the garden season.

All of these projects are how-to's for an audience interested in improving their homes and taking care of their cars.

Cosmopolitan uses a several-pronged theme that translates generally to: *how to be sexy and find men . . . How to be a glamorous, healthy woman in a modern world . . . what you need to know to be a smart, up-to-date, modern woman.* Now let's look at some of the article titles and see how they fit this focus.

How to be sexy and find men:

- " 'Shopping for a Mate: Video Dating' (One single girl's futuristic manhunt—via TV monitor!)"
- " 'What Makes You Say Yes to a Man' (To have sex or not?)"
- " 'What's It Like to Live in San Diego?' (Where you can find super jobs, super men!)"
- " 'High Sexual Anxiety: What We Fear Most in Relationships' (How to chase worries that spoil amour)."

How to be glamorous in a modern world:

- "The Joys of Not Being a Slob"
- " 'How to be a MINI Magician' (Even problem legs can pass muster in a miniskirt)."

What you need to know to be a smart, up-to-date modern woman:

- "Job Hunting by Mail" (Employers do it in "Help Wanted" ads; you can do it, by letter.)
- " 'Learn to Write a Super Cover Letter' (This could be the start of a beautiful career)."
- " 'Who's Afraid of the Big Bad Bank? Not You!' (How to melt those frosty fiscal folks)."

- " 'New Discoveries about Depression' (Revolutionary therapies to banish the 'mean blues')."

Each magazine has a focus and the articles it runs reflect that focus. Some magazines have a stronger direction than others. I used *Cosmopolitan* as an example because its focus is so clear and direct that you can't miss it. With some magazines you'll have to study carefully to discern a real focus. But they all have it. And once you become aware of this, you will be able to target every article you write directly to a magazine.

HOW TO FIND A MAGAZINE'S FOCUS

To discover a magazine's focus you will need to study at least six issues carefully. The more popular magazines can be found at your local library; larger libraries will have some of the less popular ones as well. In practice, I pick six issues from the preceding twelve months. If you want to be completely up-to-date, however, examine the last six issues. Now, do some studying.

Look at the cover.   Who is it aimed at? And what does the cover say about the magazine? *Cosmopolitan,* for instance, always features a flamboyantly and often elegantly dressed "modern" woman in a sexy pose. Covers usually tell more about a magazine than any other single feature.

Read the ads.   Who are they meant for? If you look at a few from *Cosmo* you find a woman dressed in a bra standing in the midst of elegantly dressed women. The caption says, "The Maidenform Woman. You Never Know Where She'll Turn Up." Another one shows an elegant woman, dressed in furs, with the caption, "She's Not Going to Marry the Boy Next Door."

Obviously, these two ads are aimed at a hip, young, fairly fashion-conscious working woman. Any articles you submitted would have to be aimed at this same woman.

On the other hand, in another magazine I found an ad that shows two healthy, smiling couples in bathing suits frolicking around a pool. There are palm trees and boats in the background. The caption says, "Live the Wish-Bone Lifestyle. Living the Wish-Bone lifestyle means eating right, feeling right, and getting the right kind of exercise."

Obviously this ad is targeted to robust, alive people in their late twenties to the early forties who are concerned about their health and well-being. Many of the other ads in this magazine reflect the same focus. Articles submitted here would be aimed at both men and women interested in living a healthy lifestyle.

See chapter 6, page 109, for a detailed discussion of how to translate the format of ads like these into demographic data you can use to specifically target a reader.

Read the editorial.   In her column, "Step into My Parlor," *Cosmo* editor Helen Gurley Brown talks about such subjects as women in power; how a flat stomach separates the sexy-looking girl from the one who may be, but has to prove it; and making love with passion. This editorial column gives an excellent idea of how *Cosmo* looks at its world, and how you have to look at it too if you intend to please the *Cosmo* editors.

Read the columns.   If you look at the column "Analyst's Couch" in *Cosmo,* you'll find questions like this: "I've been happily married for ten years, but for the past eight I've been having an affair with a man—also married—I met on a business trip. The relationship gives both of us great pleasure and no one's being hurt. Is adultery always harmful?" Other columns have a similar focus.

Read the letters to the editor.   In a letter to *Cosmopolitan* a reader talks about being offended by an article on the "roadies" that follow rock musicians and goes on to describe the difference between a roadie and a groupie. The letters to *Cosmopolitan's* editor simply reinforce our original idea of *Cosmo.*

Look at the article titles and the pictures.   In a recent issue, *Cosmo* ran "The Secrets of Sexual Chemistry." The picture has a woman lying full-length on top of a man on a couch. Her forehead is against his. "The Dynamics of Drive" features a powerful, well-dressed businesswoman with a briefcase. "The New (and Surprising!) Facts about Sex" shows a man and a woman in bathing suits. She's shaving his chest with a razor and he has his hand on her knee. Each of these gives a clear picture of exactly what the magazine feels its readers want to read and see.

Read the articles.   This is the least important part of the exercise, because by this time you already have an excellent idea of the magazine's focus. But it helps give you a grasp of the approach, the style, and the language used by the publication.

At this point you are well on your way to really understanding the point of view (focus) the magazine feels it must take to reach its readers.

With this understanding you can start to create article ideas that will appeal to the magazine's readers and to the editor who is looking for articles to fit that particular magazine's focus.

UNDERSTANDING MAGAZINE CATEGORIES

Once you feel you know one magazine's point of view well, you should move on to try to understand exactly what categories of articles the magazine takes. The editorial content of each magazine, as already explained, is designed to reach and meet the needs of that magazine's readers. If you read magazines regularly, you'll discover rather quickly that certain magazines offer the same general topics to their readers month after month. Sometimes they break them out for you in the table of contents.

With some magazines the table of contents heads and the categories are synonymous. Other magazines generalize a number of categories into a broad classification like "Lifestyle." In many cases, determining categories is a matter of looking through several issues of a magazine and trying to see what general subjects most of the articles can be classified into. Now let's take a look at *Woman's Day* and *Family Circle.*

Woman's Day seems to run the most articles in the following areas: "Food and Nutrition," "Parenting and Kids," "Your Looks," "Money Management and Finance," "Your Home," "Health and Fitness," "Smart Shopping/Smart Consumer," "Family/Marriage Problems," "Careers/Jobs and Work," "Your Problems," "Antiques/Crafts," "True-Life Drama," "Women's Well Being/Women's Concerns," and "Improving Your Life as a Woman."

Family Circle uses articles in the same categories, plus a couple more: "Current Events," and "Your Auto." They also do crossovers. That is, they include short articles from several categories under blanket titles such as "The Cold Weather Survival Guide." Under this section they cover topics like "Winterize your Health" and "Cold Weather Beauty." These categories are similar to those used by *Woman's Day,* but there are some differences.

For instance, if you had an article idea about automobiles or driving that would interest women, you would probably send it to *Family Circle,* not *Woman's Day,* which seldom carries automotive articles of any kind. Obviously *Family Circle* would not be interested in technical automotive articles; it wants car information that would be useful to women. This might include the following titles: "Car Repair Tips from the Pros," "Best Car Buys" (with an emphasis on women's needs), and "You Need A Tune Up, Lady."

In major women's magazines much of the food, fashion, and sometimes home building and remodeling are handled by the staff or someone assigned by the staff. These sections generally are difficult to break into, but it's not impossible. Most of the other topics found in these magazines are wide open. In the beginning I'd suggest you avoid the largely staff-written food (recipes, not nutrition), fashion, and homebuilding sections for the major women's magazines and concentrate on the other areas.

FINDING THE COMMON DENOMINATOR

You might feel that if you prepare an article for one magazine it would automatically go to the others within the field without change. Not true.

You will find that magazines not only look at the world differently and publish in particular categories, each one also approaches the articles within each of these categories from a different point of view than its competitors do.

First, let's look at some of the *Woman's Day* articles under the major classifications. Here they are from six issues.

Food and nutrition. "Microwave Cooking Poultry and Meats," "Beautiful Breads with Half the Work," "Big Time Taste on a Small Scale," and "Cooking For One or Two."

Parenting and kids. "Helping an Unpopular Child" and "Single Parent? Here's How to Make Christmas Merry . . . When It's Just You and the Kids."

Your looks.   "Anchorwomen: Looking Great All the Time" and "How to Have the Best Skin Ever."

Money management and finance.   "When Families Fight Over Money" and "How Not to Lose Friends Over Money."

Your home.   "How We Made Two Homes from One," "A Space in the Sun: Rooms that let you garden indoors and provide heat for the rest of the house," "Fencing with Charm: A Guide to Shopping for Fences," and "Grow Your Own Green Salad."

Health and fitness.   "What You Should Know about Male Cancers," "Your Child's Health: What Parents Can Do to Lay Sleep Problems to Rest," "Cosmetic Allergies (Discover What Causes Them and What Can Be Done about Them)," "How to Stay Slim after Thirty-Five," "Fifteen Ways to Prevent Permanent Scars," "How to Keep Up Your Energy Over the Holidays," "Is Your Blood Pressure Low Enough?", and "Health Problems Vitamins Can Help Solve."

Smart shopping/smart consumer.   "If Not Satisfied, Get Your Money Back and More" and "Squeezing the Most Out of a Lemon: Don't Suffer with That New Car."

Family/marriage problems.   "When Families Fight Over Money."

Careers, jobs, and work.   "Great Ways to Earn $25,000 or More" and "Women Who've Made Millions."

Antiques/crafts.   "Do You Own a Goldmine in Old Jewelry?" and "Antiques—Best Buys for $100 or Less."

True-life drama.   "My Grandson, Home at Last," "How Do You Reason with a Duck?" "What It Takes to Raise My Jamie" (mothering a disabled child), and "Treating Trauma: Countdown Between Life and Death" (an emergency care nurse who became the victim of an auto accident).

Women's well-being/women's concerns.   "Escaping Rape: Techniques for Outsmarting Rapists."

Giving.   "Spiritual Labors of Love" (inspired church women across the country donate their time and talent to beautify their houses of worship).

LOOKING OVER THE HEALTH ARTICLES Now let's pull out the health articles and see if we can find a common denominator. First, there are two continuing series of articles written by MDs that are, therefore, not open to freelancers.

There are a few articles on health, however, that are bylined by freelancers. Look for the name of each article's author in the list of staff members and frequent contributors near the front of the magazine to determine whether the article was submitted by a freelancer.

Here are the ones I found in six issues: "How to Stay Slim After 35," "The Sensationally Simple Diet: Low Cal Meals from Packaged Foods" (written by a registered dietician), "Why You Should Learn to Love Fish" (written by an MD), and "What You Should Know About Male Cancers: Missing the symptoms of testicular and prostate cancer can mean losing out on lifesaving treatment."

If you want to sell a health article to *Woman's Day,* it is your job to figure out why these articles were purchased in the first place. That is, what is the common denominator among these articles? Three of them have something to do with diet (how to stay slim) and nutrition. The third one is about male health. If I wanted to write a health article for *Woman's Day,* I would explore diets, staying slim, and nutrition. Each would need a unique twist. How about: "Why So Many Diets Include Pasta," "A Simple Diet for Women on the Go," or "Diets for People Who Eat Out"?

Now let's look at the health category in *Family Circle.* These articles seem to cover a wider range and offer better opportunities for freelancers. Here are some titles: "Killing Your Skin and Yourself: A Must Read Before You Go Out in the Sun," "Walk Your Way to a Healthy Heart," "Sixteen Home Remedies You Can Trust," "Twenty-Two Emergency Hotlines," and "How to Winterize Your Health." These focus strongly on prevention and how-to, as contrasted to *Woman's Day*'s concentration on healthy eating for a good figure.

To come up with possible ideas within this general classification, you should focus on prevention and how-to, also. You might try such ideas as: "Sixteen Ways to Cut Down on Home Accidents" and "Low Impact Aerobics You Can Do at Home."

As you can see, a health/fitness article written for *Woman's Day* probably doesn't have much of a chance at *Family Circle.* The reverse is also true. All of these, of course, are health articles, but the approaches are distinctively different. If you intend to sell to magazines like these, you must become aware of these differences and tailor each article specifically to the magazine you intend to write for. If you are interested in writing fitness and health articles, you'll find that *How to Make Money Writing About Fitness and Health* by Celia and Tom Scully offers detailed advice.

EXAMINING INDIVIDUAL APPROACHES   Now let's leave the women's magazines and try the popular science magazines. All of them publish recreation articles, but each magazine has a different approach. Let's take a look at recreational articles in *Popular Mechanics:*

- "Barrels of Money: You'll Find Beauty, Quality, and Tradition in These Shotguns."

- "To Alaska and Back: The Alcan—a 5,000-mile Blast Through Canada."

- "High Tech Trailwear: lighter, drier, and more breathable."

- "Commemorative Firearms: They Can Bring a Sizable Return to Your Investment."

- "The Toys of Summer: *PM* Gathered Eleven Motorized Beach Toys for a Wet 'n' Wild Showdown at Disney World."

All of these articles would be interesting to an upscale male. Notice what they stress: expensive, high quality shotguns; high tech trailwear; commemorative firearms; and motorized beach toys. All of the articles except the Alcan highway piece are about collections. They're overviews of what's available, often with a focus on collecting or investing.

Now, using this common denominator, project some possible article ideas. How about upscale tents? Roughing it in style? Items that let you hit the trail with class? Upscale safaris for the man who's done everything?

Let's look at the recreational articles in *Popular Science*. Here are a few:

- "Flip Flash, Auto Focus from Kodak."

- "Sneakers that Think: Computerized Sneakers that Give You Data on How Far, How Long You've Walked and More."

- "Install a mini generator in your RV."

- "Wind Tunnel-Tuned Tennis Racket."

What's the common denominator here? Gadgets. All are brand new and different products that have something unique about them: flip flash auto focus, a new tiny generator, and computerized sneakers. To sell to this market, you would look for the unusual and the different. Possibles might be "a tent equipped with solar cells," "a backpack with a built-in walkie-talkie," or something similar.

As you can see, although *Popular Science* and *Popular Mechanics* are similar, their approach is as different as night and day.

To make an educated guess at what any magazine will buy, you must find the common denominator among the articles they publish and then approach similar topics with a unique twist.

THE FIVE-POINT MAGAZINE IDEA CHECKLIST

Here is a short checklist you can use to gauge whether your article idea might be suitable for a particular magazine.

1. *Does your idea fit the magazine's image of itself?* For instance, an article aimed at blue-collar housewives would not fit *Cosmopolitan's* image of itself.

2. *Does this article idea fit the magazine's focus?* An article on how to dress well on a budget would probably fit *Woman's Day,* but it certainly wouldn't fit *Cosmopolitan's* focus on the smart, sophisticated young woman.

3. *Does the idea fall within the categories generally taken by the magazine?* To check this, decide what category your idea

falls in, then make sure the magazine covers this particular area.

4. *Does it seem to fit the reader's lifestyle?* As you can see, magazines focus a great deal of attention on their readers' lifestyles. Articles that aren't compatible with this lifestyle are usually rejected.

5. *Does this article idea have the same common denominator as the other articles within this category?* Remember the *Popular Mechanics* and *Popular Science* example—these two magazines may take articles in the same category, but the approaches are diametrically opposed.

MONEY AND RIGHTS

Acquiring magazine savvy also means understanding how the magazines approach money and article rights. These two topics are of vital concern to every writer who is attempting to make money from his or her writing.

MONEY

Let's start again with the premise that a magazine is a business. Every magazine has a budget which allocates a fixed amount of money during the year for staff salaries, printing, editorial fees, and other expenses. This means the editor is allowed to spend only so much each year to purchase articles for the publication. The editor might spend twice what he or she intended on one particular article, but unless there is some leeway in the budget, the editor will have to cut back on the price paid for some other piece. In most cases, however, there is some room for negotiating price.

Pay rates.   Magazines generally offer a beginning writer a fairly low rate. Sometimes even a major magazine will offer five hundred dollars or less to a beginning writer for an article of 1,500 to 3,500 words. Usually they will raise the rates as you contribute more articles, but that's not always the case. I know several professional writers who complain that a few of the major magazines won't raise them much above $700.

On the other hand, I also know writers who receive $6,000 to

$7,500 per article and, in some cases, quite a bit more. Generally these amounts are paid to professionals who are well-known to the magazine or have a "name." Often too, the articles that command these rates require quite a bit of research and travel.

Negotiating your own rate. Despite the generalities about payment that we just discussed, there is always some room for negotiation with a magazine, even when making a first sale. There are basically three separate situations here:

Speculation. When you send in an article "on speculation," meaning that an editor is willing to look at it but not necessarily to buy, many magazines, especially the smaller publications, will simply send you a check for a certain amount if the article is accepted. You can accept this, or you can write back, explain why you feel the article is worth more, and state exactly what you want.

I have been successful at this most of the time. A few times, I have lost my editor over this when I inquired about payment. In one case, a trade journal paid $250 for something I had worked extremely hard to research. When I asked for more, the editor blew up and said he'd decide what to pay. When I run into someone like this, I generally mark that magazine off my list because I know, in the long run, I'll never make money working for them.

Assignment. After you have sold a few articles to a magazine, you should stop doing anything on speculation and ask to handle future articles on assignment. For assignments, all rates should be negotiated in advance. I make it a point to ask for either twenty percent above my last fee for that magazine or for about twenty percent above the rates stated in *Writer's Market.*

Price the query. Since I frequently write articles for magazines I've never worked for before, I always state the price I want at the bottom of my query. Usually I set this price at from twenty to thirty percent above the rates the magazine says they pay. Or if I have been working for similar magazines and have already established a rate, I ask for that rate, even if the magazine says it pays less.

Does this work? Or course it does. Last year I sold approximately two hundred articles to a number of magazines. All of them paid the price I asked for except one. Actually I don't use this system when working for major magazines. I simply negotiate the fee in advance. But for smaller publications it works well.

WHAT RIGHTS TO SELL

This question can be as simple or as complex as you want to make it. Here are the rights you generally sell:

First North American rights.   Generally I lump similar rights together here: first North American English language rights and North American English language rights. This gives the magazine the right to publish the article first in English in the United States and Canada. After it is published by the magazine, you are free to resell it. There are some technical differences between the two, but the outcome is the same.

Second rights.   The magazine acquires the right to publish an article that has already been published first by another magazine.

One time rights.   This can be first or second rights, but the magazine acquires the right to publish the article one time only.

English language periodical rights.   The magazine acquires all periodical rights that are published in English. You retain book rights, other non-periodical rights, and foreign rights.

World periodical rights.   This gives the publication the right to publish in magazines all over the world. These rights apply to both English and foreign translations. You, however, keep book and dramatic rights.

All rights.   The publication obtains the right to publish the material in both magazines and books. This applies to both English and foreign translations.

What you sell depends on the magazine and you. Most magazines ask for first North American rights. Some insist on world periodical rights because they have foreign editions. Others are willing to buy one time rights.

Don't give your rights away just because the magazine asks for them. The rights you retain will mean extra money to you when you resell your articles later on. The American Society of Authors and Journalists suggests that writers sell first North American publication rights only. I personally mark all manuscripts, except those intended for major magazines, "one time rights." This is usually accepted and allows me to resell my manuscript anywhere I wish.

If a magazine asks for more than first North American rights, you should always try to negotiate. Some magazines will accept the rights you offer, others will not publish your article if you don't give them the rights they ask for. If a magazine insists on world periodical rights or all rights, you should always ask for more money than they have offered. The justification is that you won't be able to make additional income by selling second rights to other magazines. Sometimes a publication will agree to pay more for additional rights, and sometimes they won't. But it doesn't hurt to ask.

Often, magazines that acquire world rights or all periodical rights will often give you your rights back after they have published your article. This is never automatic; you must always ask.

Some magazines send you a contract or a letter of agreement to sign that states the rights you are selling. Many simply send a letter stating what they will buy. Sometimes the rights the magazine wants to acquire are printed on the check. Often beginning writers will simply sign these and send them back. When you do, you have given them whatever rights they ask for. Don't sign anything until you and the magazine agree on what you are going to sell.

Work-for-hire agreements. This is primarily an agreement that commits you to write the article as an employee of the magazine. Essentially it transfers the ownership of all your rights to a magazine. This means you will not be able to sell the article more than once. A few magazines simply won't publish your article if you refuse to sign a work-for-hire agreement. In general, you should turn down these agreements.

Suppose, however, you want to see your article published in the magazine regardless of the terms. Don't just sign the work-for-hire agreement; write and ask the editor for more money. The argument is that the price they are offering is about what other magazines pay for one time rights. Therefore, if they want to buy all ownership rights they should pay more since they are limiting your potential income from this article. You won't always get more money this way, but you should try.

Expenses. Magazines won't pay expenses for work done on speculation. If a piece is assigned, the magazine should pay for telephone calls, meals, transportation and other legitimate out-of-pocket expenses. When negotiating a price with an editor, always make sure that he understands you expect expenses above and beyond the price of the article. You may be asked to submit an estimate of such expenses for the editor's OK.

Letters of agreement.   Any time an editor gives you an assignment, you should send him a letter that confirms the agreement to research and write a particular article. Include the name of the article, the agreed on delivery date, the approximate number of words, the price, and the name of the publication. Have the editor sign this and return the confirmation to you. This type of agreement helps avoid misunderstandings.

As you can see, acquiring magazine savvy gives you an insight into how a magazine sees the world, approaches its readers, generally selects the articles it publishes, and deals with its writers for money and rights. This gives you information to help you come up with ideas that will be accepted by a particular publication. And it also helps when you're trying to negotiate a fee.

2. Fitting Your Ideas to the Market

For every article idea there are literally dozens or maybe even hundreds of potential markets. The problem is that most of us as writers are market illiterates and simply won't, or don't, take the time to search for all the possibilities.

I know one writer who took a trip to Europe with the hope of selling a number of articles. There she shot hundreds of pictures, interviewed a couple dozen people, and gathered as much information as possible.

Along the way she came up with some outstanding material: the Dingle Peninsula, the Irish pubs of Dingle, walking in Churchill's footsteps, the street markets of London, the Fitzpatrick Castle/Hotel, a one-day trip to the Western Highlands of Scotland, and walking the royal mile in England. All of these are great ideas, but so far, none of them have been sold. Why? Two reasons:

The first is that she doesn't have a very good idea which magazines are interested in this type of travel material. So far she has queried such publications as *Travel and Leisure*, and *Travel-Holiday Magazine*. These are good magazines but they receive so much material and require that it be handled in such a distinct way that they are hard to hit.

Second, she hasn't studied these or other travel markets well, so she doesn't have a good understanding of what angles these and other publications take, nor how they want the material put together to appeal to their readers.

PLETHORA OF PUBLICATIONS

This writer picked the magazines she did because it was obvious they take travel pieces. That's okay, but such magazines are only the tip of the iceberg. There are hundreds of publications that are not travel publications but that will still occasionally buy travel articles. Some purchase a tremendous amount of travel material and most are easier to sell to than *Travel and Leisure.* These more general magazines are the ones you need to approach.

They represent what I call the "hidden travel market." The *Christian Science Monitor,* for instance, has run such travel or travel-related pieces as "Gallery of Imported Food Boutiques at New York Store" (a specialized gourmet imported foods department in Bloomingdale's), "Summer Festival Honors Guadeloupe Women Cooks," "The August Food Festival in Pointe-à-Pitre, Guadeloupe," (a French Caribbean island), "Planning a Tour of English Gardens" (a guide to great English gardens), "The Wonderful Vermont Country Store" (the country store in Weston, Vermont), and "Country Guest Houses in and around Grafton" (historic inns in Grafton, Vermont). All of these were travel pieces with rather special angles.

Compass, a company magazine of the Marine Office of America (a representative of several insurance companies), recently featured "Diving For Abalone" (an article about California's commercial abalone industry) and "The Orient Express Rides Again" (an article that describes the history of the famous train and a trip aboard it between Venice and London).

Modern Maturity, the official publication of the American Association of Retired Persons, recently ran an article on river rafting Utah's San Juan River and another on Death Valley. And *Friendly Exchange,* the Farmer's Insurance magazine, featured a piece on winter carnivals across the United States.

All of these are articles that almost any writer could have picked up while on vacation in any of these places. It is a matter of (1) being aware of what's going on around you, and (2) trying to find all the possible markets for this type of material.

PUTTING THE ODDS IN YOUR FAVOR

We are currently in what I call the age of the magazine. *Writer's Market* now lists over 4,000 markets. And last year witnessed the birth of 231 new magazines, including waves of science, computer, music, video, and military publications. New titles include *Grandparents, Midwest Living, Child, Parenting, Southern,* and *Automobile.*

In addition, the Educational Press Association of America now counts ninety-two magazines aimed at children thirteen years or younger. Titles here include: *Pre-K Today, Kids Club Magazine, Geoffrey's Toys R Us,* and *Sesame Street Magazine.* Name almost any subject and you can find a dozen magazines or more that cover it.

All of this provides a tremendous opportunity for writers. The problem is that it has become increasingly difficult to keep track of these magazines and especially to know what each one of them takes. For years I planned to put all the magazines and their contents in a computer, so I could give it my article idea, say "beekeeping for beginners," and the computer would come up with all possible markets.

So far, that's an impossibility; but you can put the odds in your favor if you approach marketing systematically. In this chapter, we will do just that and examine two systems that will help you to turn up a number of specific markets for each idea.

THE ARTICLE GAME

I like to make a game out of both looking for articles and searching for out-of-the-way markets. Over the years I have had good success in finding publications that will buy almost every subject I tackled.

In some cases I even surprise myself. Let's take a look at one example. A few years ago, I took a brief Sunday trip down Highway 49 in California's Mother Lode Country. This is the area where gold was discovered in California in 1848. In 1849 and the next few years after that, miners from all over the world rushed to California to strike it rich. Today the area still boasts old gold rush buildings, rusting mining equipment, an occasional stagecoach, and other relics of a bygone era.

All I did was drive about a hundred miles between Sonora and Auburn, California. Along the way, I stopped at all the old hotels, museums, historic buildings, and other points of interest. I talked to everyone who had something to say about the gold rush days. I also paid special attention to people gold panning and mining the streams for fun. I probably took several hundred pictures that day.

Then I came home and developed the pictures. I placed all the photos and other material on a large table and let them sit there for a few days. During that time, I mulled over the possibilities. Sometimes I'd come up with an angle working on some other material or just walking around the house.

Finally I sorted everything out, wrote my queries, and put the articles together as I received the go-aheads. Here are the results from that one-day trip.

- A picture story entitled "Churches Mean Christmas in California's Mother Lode" to the Sunday *San Francisco Chronicle.*

- An article "Camping California's Mother Lode" to *Camping Guide.*

- An article "Trailering California's Mother Lode" to *Trail R News*.*

- An article "Panning for Gold" (something to do while trailering the Mother Lode) to *Trailer Life.*

- An article "Gold Strike Trailer Park," (an unusual trailer park) to *Trailer Topics*.*

- "Skin Diving for Gold" to *Ford Truck Times.*

*No longer published.

- "Skin Diving for Gold" to *Skin Diver Magazine.*
- A reprint of the *Ford Truck Times* story in *My Weekly Reader.*
- "California's Mother Lode" to the *Kansas City Star.*

How did I find this many markets? It's easy. Here are the available marketing directories and the system I used.

THE MARKET DIRECTORIES

There are a number of market directories you will need to use in your search to find all possible markets for your article idea. Here are the major ones. See the Bibliography for full citations of these and other important books.

Writer's Market. This is the writer's bible and the one you will find most generally useful. If I were going to buy only one market directory, this would be it.

Standard Rate and Data. This comes in several volumes. The ones of interest to writers are: *Consumer Magazines* (such as *Reader's Digest* and *Family Circle*), *Business Publications* (such as *Fishing Tackle Trade News* and *Shooting Industry*), *Newspapers,* and *Newsletters.* Generally this includes the name and address of the publication, the editorial policy, and the name of the publication's editor.

Editor and Publisher International Year Book. This directory lists American and foreign daily newspapers.

Working Press of the Nation, Vol. 5. This volume covers company, organization, and group publications. It includes magazines like *Ford Times, Compass* and *The Cententer* (the Halliburton Services magazine). These magazines make an excellent and often overlooked market for freelancers.

Religious Writer's Marketplace. This gives details about the Christian publications. If you are a Christian writer, you need this one in your library.

Ulrich's International Periodicals Directory. This is a complete survey of all international markets, including newspapers, business publications, consumer magazines, and others. It is a must if you intend to write for the global market.

Most of these publications are available at the reference desk of your local library.

FINDING TWENTY TO THIRTY MARKETS FOR EACH IDEA

Believe it or not, there are at least twenty possible markets for each article idea. The trick, of course, is to find them.

Over the years, in classes, we have developed a very simple, but effective, procedure using the *Writer's Market.* I want to offer it here, and show you exactly how it works.

Start with the idea.   If I take the subject of the gold country and gold panning, I ask myself first who would be interested. The answer would be: a lot of general readers, recreational vehicle owners, outdoorsmen, adventurers, women who like the outdoors, campers, teenagers, children, and retirees.

Go through the table of contents of *Writer's Market.*   Ask yourself which magazine categories might be interested in your article idea? Here is the list I felt might work with my gold country idea.

Association, Club	Newspapers
Automotive	Regional
General	Retirement
Health and Fitness	Science
Hobby and Craft	Sports
In-Flight	Travel
Juvenile	Women's
Men's	

In making out your list, don't cross off any group automatically; try to look at the bigger picture. Within a particular category or group of magazines you will find a lot of individual variation. Within the Automotive and Motorcycle section, for instance, you'll find such magazines as *Autoweek, Car and Driver, Four Wheeler,* and *Friends.*

The standard automotive magazines, such as *Autoweek,* and *Car and Driver,* are technically automotive-oriented and wouldn't be interested in our gold country piece. *Four-Wheeler,* on the other hand, sometimes takes articles about back country off-the-road activities, and that's what gold panning (a gold country recreational activity) can be. *Friends Magazine,* published for Chevrolet owners, sometimes buys travel and travel-related pieces. And, of course, the gold country would be an interesting destination for a Chevrolet family, and gold panning could well be a fun, family-oriented activity.

List all possibilities.   If there is any chance that even one magazine within a category might be interested in your article idea, put that category on your "possible" list. At first glance, the women's group doesn't seem to offer any possibility. But they take so many things that it's worth exploring.

It also doesn't seem as if association magazines would be interested, but within that classification you find such publications as *California Highway Patrolman* and *Elks Magazine. California Highway Patrolman* sometimes takes California travel. *Elks Magazine* runs many articles on interesting topics. Other categories also contain such a wide variety of magazines, which take such varied topics, that you must consider each table of contents listing carefully.

Read the descriptions of individual magazines under each section.   Ask yourself which ones might be interested in your idea, and make a list of them.

Here is the list I made for the gold country/gold panning piece:

Association, Club, and Fraternal
California Highway Patrolman
Catholic Forester
D.A.C. News
Kiwanis
Perspective
Woodman of the World

Automotive
Four Wheeler
Friends
Nissan Discovery
Volkswagen's World

General Interest
The American Legion Magazine
Caper's Weekly

Ford Times
Friendly Exchange
Globe
Lefthander Magazine
National Geographic
The Star

Health and Living
Bruce Jenner's Better
Health and Living

Hobby and Craft
Lost Treasure
Western & Eastern Trea-
sures

In-Flight
Western World

Men's
Cavalier
Gent
Saga

Newspapers
The San Francisco Chron-
icle
The Los Angeles Times

The Denver Post
The Kansas City Star

Regional
Bakersfield Lifestyle
California Magazine
Sierra Life Magazine

Retirement
Modern Maturity
Prime Times
Silver Circle

Science
Home Mechanix
Popular Science
Popular Mechanics

Sports
Skin Diver
Field and Stream
Outdoor Life
Sports Afield
Western Outdoors

Women's
Woman's Day
Family Circle

Would different articles based on the general topics of gold panning, finding gold, or the gold country itself sell to every one of these magazines? Of course not. But because I found an individual angle for each magazine that would appeal to its readers, I sold to some of them; in fact, more than I expected.

Patiently sifting through all the possible markets led me to literal gold: a succession of checks in my mailbox.

PUTTING MULTIPLE MARKETING KNOW-HOW TO WORK

After doing so well with the gold country/gold panning article, I began putting this system to work both for myself and my writing classes. Over the years I have had tremendous success with it. Some of the ideas I tried, at first glance, didn't seem to offer many possibilities. But most turned out far better than I expected.

A few years ago, I spotted a clipping in the newspaper about Indians adding camping and recreational facilities on their reservations to attract tourists and raise money. I put this idea through the *Writer's Market* system and came up with a list of fifty-six magazines that might take this subject.

I have to admit this surprised me, but I still didn't have any inkling of this idea's potential. I then came up with a title slanted into each magazine and sent the queries. Here are the results: "Indian Reservation Adventure" to *Argosy**, "Fishing and Hunting the Indian Reservations" to *Sports Afield*, "Try a Luxury Vacation on an Indian Reservation" to *McCall's,* "Boating the Indian Reservations" to *Outdoors,* "Fifteen Indian Reservations to Visit This Summer" to *Better Homes and Gardens,* "Take Your Trailer to an Indian Reservation" to *Trailer Life,* and "Camping the Indian Reservations" to *Camping Guide*.*

I think I could have made more sales on this subject, but I got tired of the idea and stopped querying.

THE MULTIPLE AUDIENCE/INTEREST METHOD

In addition to the *Writer's Market* system offered here for finding multiple markets by going through the categories one by one, there is another method that works well. Simply start with the idea, then consider the wide range of "audiences" that might be interested. Here are some tips that will help.

*No longer published.

CONSIDER AN INDIVIDUAL'S AFFILIATIONS When you're writing a personality piece, for instance, try to determine what business that person is in, what church he goes to, and what clubs or organizations he belongs to. If he is a Rotarian and is doing something really unusual, try the *Rotarian* magazine. The same principle applies for the *Optimist* magazine, *Kiwanis* magazine, and others.

Supposing the person you've interviewed is Presbyterian, try *Presbyterian Record* and *Presbyterian Survey;* Lutheran, the *Lutheran Journal;* and so on.

TAP THE EXPERIENCE RANGE Suppose you're interviewing an outstanding personality and discover he houseboats, skin dives, vacations in an RV, rides a motorcycle, or owns a 4-wheel drive vehicle. In this case, you may well have articles for magazines that focus on each of these interests, provided that you connect it solidly with the individual sport, as I did with my gold country article for *Skin Diver Magazine.*

THINK MANUFACTURER INTEREST Whenever you're doing a story, consider the equipment that your people are using. If you're writing an article on a tree farm, and they're using International Harvester equipment, query the International Harvester publications. You will find a complete list of company publications in the *Working Press of the Nation,* Volume 5.

CONSIDER AGE DIFFERENCES Consider different age categories: The retirement field today is bigger than ever before and growing. Here you find such magazines as *50 Plus, Golden Years, Mature Living, Mature Years, Modern Maturity, Prime Time, Silver Circle,* and *3 Score and 10.* Perhaps that article idea you have on shopping in Europe might appeal to one of these.

Or let's say you're working on an article about banking. Could children be interested in this? They certainly wouldn't want to read about one particular bank, but they might have an interest in the world of banking in general, slanted toward that age group's concerns.

The teen market also is wide open. Some of the magazines focus heavily on the rock music scene, but others such as *Live for Teens* and *Campus Life* take career, travel projects and activities, and many other topics.

TRY ROUNDUPS   A "roundup" article is one that surveys or collects a number of similar things or examples along a single theme. I might, for instance, write an article on gourmet fast food restaurants of Northern California. In it I would survey and write about a number of representative fast food restaurants (maybe ten to twelve), or perhaps I would write an article called "Ten Short Bicycle Trips to Take." The article would then simply be a "roundup" or a collection of ten trips.

This category doesn't consider the interest range of the audience or the magazine, but often after you have sold eight to ten articles based on audience interest, you can write a roundup using the examples or subjects from the other articles. For instance, after you have sold several personality articles on retirees, you might do a roundup on retirees in politics, ten seniors who've made it big after retirement, or something similar.

SEARCH SYSTEMATICALLY   The audience/interest method works best if you systematically break a subject down into its basic parts. Let's say you have decided you'd like to write an article on a wagon train that goes on an annual trek into the mountains each summer. The first step is to find out as much about this wagon train as possible. Collect newspaper articles on the subject or call the sponsor and ask.

Maybe you discover that this particular fifteen-day trip is sponsored by a church group in Colorado and has from ten to fifteen wagons. The participants come from six states and include families with children and pets, a number of old-timers, selected underachieving high school students and others. Several teachers within the group conduct nature studies at various places along the way.

BREAK IT DOWN   Now take a pencil and paper and break out the basic elements: Religious organization, Colorado, people from several areas, children, pets, retirees, pioneering, and teaching program for underachievers.

Articles based on this wagon train might be sold to a variety of religious magazines, depending on the denomination of the participants, and to a regional magazine. The child angle could be offered to several age groups of juvenile magazines. It could spotlight the older members and be sent to retirement magazines. The teaching program for underachievers might have a market at women's and general publications, and at magazines and trade journals directed at the teaching profession. Since these people have come from diverse geographical areas, you may be able to interest a number of newspapers.

As a final effort, I would run each of these classifications through the *Writer's Market* system to develop the maximum number of possibilities.

RESELLING THE SAME MATERIAL MANY TIMES

Once you have found a number of possible markets for your broad general idea, you need to (1) determine what angle of the broad general subject that magazine might like, (2) organize a separate article around the angle you have selected for each magazine, and (3) write a different article for each magazine. The only thing that's the same about each of these articles is that you are going to use many of the same facts and the same information in all of them.

You can also sell a single article to a number of different magazines. That, however, is an entirely different process and will be covered in detail in chapter 7.

Here are the steps you need to go through to sell articles based on the same basic material to a number of different publications.

1. List magazines that might be interested in your subject. Use the methods already described in this chapter.

2. Send for the magazines. Once you have a list of possible markets, send for every one of them. I know writers who never look at the magazine they intend to query. They simply guess at what these magazines might like. These people sometimes sell a few articles, but they aren't the ones who make consistent sales. Those writers who do are the ones who study the magazines carefully before they write a query letter.

I urge you to build a magazine library. I find it's impossible to know what these magazines take unless you actually have copies to look at. Check *Writer's Market* and send for every magazine within your area of interest that you can't buy on the newsstand. I have had students send for all those non-newsstand magazines listed in this publication. I personally have about a thousand that I scan regularly.

Generally publishers won't give you magazines like *Newsweek* and *TV Guide,* which are readily available for public sale. But the several thousand publishers whose publications are available only by mail will usually send you one or several copies to look over.

I ask my students to mail a postcard with a message that says, "Please send me a sample copy of your magazine and guidelines for writers, if available." Whenever I recommend this in class I always get an argument from those who insist that they must enclose postage or, in some cases, money for the magazine. Some magazines, of course, ask for this. In practice, I find it isn't necessary.

Many magazines list their policies about sending sample copies in *Writer's Market.* No matter what they state, however, I suggest that you send a request to every magazine on your list (with the statement already mentioned). In practice, I find that the postcard request works in eighty-five to ninety percent of all cases. When this method stops bringing results, then I'll have the class try something else. Right now, don't waste your money sending stamps or money. If you want to be absolutely sure you won't be charged for a sample copy, state, "Please send me a free sample copy and writer's guidelines if available."

3. Study the magazines carefully. When you receive the sample copies, study each magazine as we did in chapter 1. Concentrate on the focus of the magazine, the categories each takes, and the common denominator that runs through the articles within similar categories. I usually recommend that writers study a minimum of six issues of each magazine. This applies primarily to major magazines you find in the library because magazine publishers will not give you this many free copies.

Even if you only have one issue to look at, however, the differences will soon become obvious. If you were to write a query on gold and gold panning for *Friendly Exchange,* the Farmer's Insurance magazine, you might propose a 1,000- to 1,500-word article that emphasizes briefly the background of what's happening, explains how the family can enjoy panning, and points out possible places to go.

For *National Geographic,* you would propose a more extensive piece of about four thousand to six thousand words, which explores what's happening all over the Mother Lode, details the reasons behind the current gold rush boom, and gives full examples of some operations. In short, you would offer an in-depth article on the subject.

The other magazines would demand similar special treatments. At least they would if you expect to get a fair share of go-aheads.

4. Decide on an angle each magazine on your list might want. This involves, as we've already seen, understanding that magazine's needs, then slanting the idea to match those needs. This is the basic process I went through in target slanting the gold country article.

For *Trailer Life,* I knew that they liked recreational ideas for trailerists—for instance, things they could do while traveling in their recreational vehicles. The magazine had already run articles on cave exploring, clamming, and similar activities, so why not gold panning?

For *Skin Diver,* I knew they liked unusual skin diving stories, so a story about a group that was conducting an unusual underwater hunt for gold seemed like a natural.

For *Ford Truck Times,* I knew they published articles on outdoor adventure if the principals in the story were using a Ford truck.

With the *San Francisco Chronicle,* I knew, from observing the Sunday edition of the magazine, that they often published visual gold country stories, especially if you could come up with an unusual angle. I decided that by tying Christmas to these picturesque churches in the Mother Lode, I would have the right angle.

I knew the camping magazine liked camping activities with a historical travel angle, so camping the Mother Lode was a natural.

This whole process I call "target slanting."

Learning to target slant: Once you start becoming acquainted with the magazines and begin to understand target slanting, you can become quite sophisticated at making educated guesses about which article ideas a magazine will actually take.

All you really need to know is that a magazine idea consists of a subject and an angle. Then you take your subject and select the appropriate angle for each magazine. Let's take the subject of the Tylenol poisonings and try it.

For this experiment, we'll try the following magazines: *Baby Talk, Popular Science, Psychology Today,* and *Drug Topics.* When you target slant, consider what you know about that magazine's focus, categories, and common denominators.

Baby Talk is a magazine geared to parents with babies and small children. A possible angle might be "Protecting Your Child from Random Poisoning."

Popular Science is the magazine that looks for what's new in science and technology. A good working angle for this magazine would be "New Package Protection for Drugs."

Psychology Today is most interested in the psychological approach to a subject. The angle here would be "Why the Tylenol Poisoning Took Place and the Tylenol Poisoning Personality."

Drug Topics is a business magazine for drug stores that is interested in helping these retailers make more money. The angle here would be: "How the Tylenol Poisoning Affected the Over-the-Counter Drug Business."

Using this process, you can target slant any topic to any magazine.

The backside twist: Sometimes finding the angle which will appeal to the magazine's readership and to the editor takes a lot of head scratching. Once in a while I have to turn what I call "conceptual backflips" to make a particular subject work. If you keep at it long enough, however, you will eventually be able to sell every idea you create.

For instance, I used to write a lot of trade journal articles. These are articles for magazines that go to people in the retail business. Here you will find such titles as *Hardware Merchandiser, Western Outfitter, Yarn Market News,* and *RV Business.* The aim of these magazines is to help particular retailers do a better job with their businesses. As a result, trade journals take articles on merchandising, advertising, security, employee training, and similar retail-related subjects.

At one time I became extremely good at figuring out what the magazines were looking for and at turning the angle to make any subject fit any magazine. As a matter of fact, I used to brag that I could go into any store, take a few pictures of anything, and come up with an angle some magazine would buy.

Well, a fellow magazine journalist Frank Zdy accepted this challenge. He said he would take me to a nursery, but he knew I wouldn't find a single idea there I could sell. I couldn't wait. When we arrived, I found the nursery was out of business. The door was off the hinges. The bricks in the patio area had been torn up. Cans were scattered everywhere, and the benches were broken.

I don't have to tell you I was discouraged. But I took a couple of dozen pictures and went home to think. What could I find that a magazine might buy? These publications, I reasoned, want to help their readers increase the dollar volume of the reader's business.

Conversely, they probably would take an article on how not to lose business. This nursery could be a bad example.

I then built the query and article around the idea that you've got to keep your physical surroundings in tip-top shape. A few months later, the story appeared in *Southern Florist and Nurseryman* under the title "How to Turn a $100,000 Investment into a Shoe-string."

5. Write your first batch of queries.   From nine to twelve publications should be selected from different categories. That is, you can send one query to the sports magazines, another to the trailer magazines, another to the automotive group, and still another to the women's magazines. These categories need not be the same as those listed in *Writer's Market*.

The key here is non-competing. You can query several magazines at a time in non-competing categories. For instance, magazines published by Ford and Chevrolet for the owners of their cars might be considered automotive magazines. But they probably wouldn't be competing for readers with the off-the-road vehicle magazines. So you could tailor one article for *Ford Times* and another, using the same research material, for *Four Wheeler*.

When you finish writing the articles from the go-aheads you received from the first group, then pick out twelve more and mail these out. I suggest twelve because this will help insure that you don't receive too many go-aheads at one time. I'm sure you would like to have this problem. But I've seen beginning writers send out fifty queries, receive twenty go-aheads, then have trouble turning out the articles in a reasonable time.

What about competing magazines? It is my opinion that a writer should be able to query two or more competing magazines at the same time. I have had students who have done this with some success. One had a true-life drama that seemed to be of interest to the women's magazines.

Being a new writer, he queried both *Ladies Home Journal* and *McCall's*. Both gave him go-aheads to do the piece on speculation and mentioned a $1,500 fee. He called *Ladies Home Journal* and told them he had a go-ahead from another magazine, but he would write it for them if they gave him a firm assignment. He then phoned *McCall's* and said he intended to write the piece for *Ladies Home Journal*. *McCall's* said they really wanted the article and would pay him $2,500 for it.

As a result he sold the piece to *McCall's*. Although the editor at *Ladies Home Journal* was upset, she did give this writer another assignment at a later date, but warned him not to do it again.

The running controversy. From a writer's point of view, simultaneously querying competing magazines with the same idea is extremely fair. Editors will tell you it's unprofessional and unethical. But remember, an editor sees only the magazine's side.

At the present time, writers have to accept basically whatever a magazine wants to pay. They also have to query competing magazines one at a time. If the article is rejected at the first magazine, a writer must go on to another magazine. This often takes up to two months at each magazine.

Sometimes a writer will spend a year or more sending his or her article to only six competing magazines. The odds in this business would be a lot more even and the pay better if magazines had to compete with each other.

Some magazines, of course, permit multiquerying as a general policy as long as the writer indentifies the query as *simultaneous* (see chapter 6 for a complete discussion of the query format). Many of these magazines list this fact in *Writer's Market*. Others object adamantly to multiquerying. Often the market guides will tell you which magazines allow it and which don't.

I personally think multiquerying should become standard practice at all magazines, whether they accept the practice or not.

I hope in the future more writers will experiment and see just how far they can push the magazines in this direction. But I must advise you to be cautious here unless you're prepared to be banned from submitting to a particular magazine or magazines.

6. Do your research. Once you have a few go-aheads, you will begin to see just how much research you have to do. Let's say we had go-aheads from *Baby Talk* for the angle "Protecting Your

Child from Random Poisoning," *Popular Science* for the angle
"New Package Protection for Drugs," *Psychology Today* for the
angle "Why the Tylenol Poisoning Took Place and the Tylenol
Poisoning Personality," and *Drug Topics* for the angle "How the
Tylenol Poisoning Affected the Over-The-Counter Drug Busi-
ness."

For the *Baby Talk* article, I might start at the local poison control
center and then obtain from the Government some overall information on protecting children from accidental poisoning. Then I
would collect the names of some national authorities on the subject from whom I could seek interviews.

For this article I would also need to talk to some people at the
pharmaceutical companies about the new packaging. While doing
this, I would also pick up the material from them for my *Popular
Science* article.

In addition, I would ask these same companies to talk about the
effect on the over-the-counter drug business. Then I would talk to
psychologists for the *Psychology Today* article. Finally, I would talk
to some drug chains and small drug stores to obtain the retailer's
angle on the over-the-counter drug business.

Each of these interviews would add different material. Some of
the material from each group of interviews might well find its way
into every article. A druggist, for instance, might have some insight
into the personality of the person who did this, some thoughts
about new packaging, and also some thoughts about protecting
children. Each person interviewed would contribute something.
When I'm finished, I'm going to have enough information to do a
lot more than four articles.

7. Write the articles.   When you finish the research, then
write the articles for the magazines that gave you go-aheads.
Again, each article should have a completely different structure
and look at the basic material in a different way from the others.
Each is a completely separate article, not the same article with a
few paragraphs changed.

If I, for instance, intended to write the *Popular Science* Tylenol
article titled "New Package Protection for Drugs," I might organize
it like this:

- Why the old packaging didn't work.
- Problems in designing new packaging.
- A case history of the new packaging.
- Types of packaging now available.
- Just how safe are these packages?
- What's in the future for packaging.

In writing this, I will dig into the packaging side of the problem. Now I send this off and start on the *Psychology Today* piece titled "Why the Tylenol Poisoning Took Place and the Tylenol Poisoning Personality." I would probably use some of my packaging information, but primarily I'm going to have to look at a much broader issue and my structure might be something like this:

- The psychological climate.
- The pressure to act.
- Why certain individuals want revenge.
- Why the original packaging made over-the-counter drugs a natural target.
- The personality profile.
- The types of individuals subject to this pressure.
- Prevention methods based on this profile.

As you can see, I am going to have to write an entirely different article. The two articles will overlap somewhat when I talk about packaging in point four, but otherwise there isn't much similarity.

Where I save time is in the fact that the research for all the Tylenol pieces can be done at one time and the overall subject is basically the same. The same will be true for the other articles within this and all other sequences.

8. Keep records. Note in a log or notebook when the article went out, the title, when it was returned or purchased, and how much was paid. If the particular article comes back, go to the next magazine on your list, read similar articles and see if you think you need to make changes to make it acceptable to that magazine.

It is possible then to sell one idea to many magazines. Sometimes the system or systems outlined in this chapter have proved so successful that my students have spent months writing dozens of articles on a single subject. For a while I thought one woman was going to make a career out of writing articles on model trains, and another sold so many pieces on Monarch butterflies that even I began to get tired of the subject. Give the methods outlined here a try and make them work for you.

3. How to Fit Your Experience to a Magazine's Needs

Over the years I have discovered that most writers, at least most beginning writers, like to start with the idea, as we did in the last chapter and then try to find the market for this idea or finished article. Frequently beginning writers will rush up to me at one of my writing seminars and say, "I've got this great article idea, now where can I sell it?"

One man, I remember quite well, had written a complete article on his canoe trip to Minnesota. What he wanted me to tell him was what magazine would buy this article without changes.

A lady in the same group had taken a raft trip down the Colorado River, then wrote an article about how the raft dragged her down-river, mostly underwater. She also wanted to know what editor would buy it just as it was.

Both seemed terribly disappointed when I told them I didn't think either article would sell unless they slanted for a particular magazine. I have always believed that starting with the idea first, then trying to find a magazine to buy it, is backwards, like making a whole suit and then trying to find someone it will fit.

What all of us as writers need to understand is that any individual article idea we come up with is not all that important. There are literally thousands of good ideas out there everywhere. Every one of us has an experience bank with thousands of pieces of information that could easily become articles.

ARTICLE IDEAS ARE EVERYWHERE

For instance, you may have shopped in a unique store, seen articles in the paper about people who do unusual things, fished in a high mountain lake, gone houseboating, taken a fascinating class, or overheard an interesting conversation. All of these represent possible article ideas. But trying to find markets after you have created the ideas is the difficult way of going about it.

Let's say your idea is "How a Drip Watering System Works." In putting this article together you go into considerable detail about the parts you need and how the system fits together. Perhaps when you finish writing, you have a good article, but it may not be slanted to meet the needs of any particular magazine.

MARKETING MISTAKES

First, you send it to *Popular Science*. Now this magazine might possibly buy an article on drip watering, but as we saw in chapter 2, articles in that magazine are designed to show off the newest and latest. So your article comes back quickly.

Next, you mail it to *Home Mechanix*. But again, *Home Mechanix* takes the how-to-do-it approach, not how it works. Therefore, if you expect to sell it, you're going to have to reslant the piece to "How to Install a Drip Watering System That Will Save You Time and Work" or something similar.

Obviously, if you've already solidified your idea, you're not going to hit either magazine. What you have to do is find the magazines that might be interested in drip watering, then target slant your basic idea to fit each of the magazines. As we saw in chapter 2, that's a lot of work. There is, however, an easier way that works almost automatically nearly every time.

MARKETING FROM THE MAGAZINE'S POINT-OF-VIEW

The easiest way to sell one particular magazine is to consider that magazine without a preconceived idea in mind of a topic or approach. You then go through the publication carefully trying to decide what experience or experiences you already have that this editor might buy. This is the basic concept. Now let's go through the individual steps and see how they work.

Decide which magazines you would like to sell an article to right now. I might base this primarily on how much a magazine pays, but usually I pick a magazine that gives me a good feeling. I ask myself two questions. Do I enjoy reading the magazine, and do I feel that I could write similar articles in that magazine's style?

When I first read *Trailer Life* magazine years ago, I said to myself that I liked the way this magazine put its articles together. I also had the feeling I could produce many just like them. I sold them the first article I tried and went on to sell two or three hundred articles over the next several years.

On the other hand, *Westways,* the magazine of the Automobile Club of Southern California, gave me just the opposite feeling. The travel subjects they bought were the same in many ways as the travel articles used by *Trailer Life,* yet I simply didn't like their approach. As a result, I was never able to sell to this magazine. That was okay, however, because there were plenty of publications out there that I really did like and understand.

Go through each magazine carefully and let the articles suggest additional ideas. Categorize each article by type and note the angle or approach the magazine uses.

Explore your own information data bank for the categories represented by each article. An information data bank is simply the information you already have available. You may have obtained this by taking a class, by working at a job, by making a clipping file, by writing other articles on the subject, or in any number of ways.

In truth, each of us already has a great deal of information already at our fingertips. Many times with a new article you will need to do some additional research. But if you also try to work in areas that you are already familiar with, you will find these articles much easier to do.

To tap your inner data bank, look at each article title, and ask yourself (1) Do I have any interest in this article and this category? (2) Do I have any special knowledge of this subject area through classes or experience? (3) Have I collected any information on this or similar subjects? (4) Could I do this or similar articles with the information I already have available? If you can answer yes to all of these questions, you should be able to easily write similar articles within the same general category.

Using the material from your own data bank, apply a similar angle to create a number of article ideas that the magazine might buy. In practice, you can do most of this mentally. Make a written note, however, of any ideas you generate so you can query later.

MAGAZINE IDEA CREATION

Now let's go through two magazines article-by-article to see just how this is done.

ANALYSIS OF MAGAZINE ONE   The following articles were taken from *Modern Maturity,* a publication of the American Association of Retired Persons. The magazine is written for a readership of persons 50 years of age or older. It generally takes articles in the following areas: historical, how-to, humor, informational, inspirational, interview, nostalgia, and personal experience handled in a special way. Here is the rundown as I went through trying to come up with possible articles I could do for the magazine.

Article 1.   "New Look in Savings Bonds." An examination from an investment standpoint of the Series EE U.S. savings bonds. The category here is *financial investment.*

Tapping your experience data bank: I have very little interest in financial matters and almost no knowledge of this subject. Therefore I would never attempt an article in this area.

Possible spin-offs: This piece, written from a "you standpoint," would appeal to retirees interested in financial investment. The subject here, savings bonds, might suggest, to another author with greater financial knowledge, possible articles on *mutual funds* or the *general bond market.*

Article 2. "Outlook for Peace." A distinguished observer assesses the prospects for East-West cooperation. This is a serious international affairs article.

Tapping your experience data bank: This also is something I don't know much about and wouldn't care to try.

Possible spin-offs: The magazine might be open to other international affairs articles, but I can't come up with a good angle.

Article 3. "Attitude Adjustment: That's the Course You Steer on a River-Raft Trip." This article chronicles a raft trip down the San Juan River in Utah and explains why the trip is so adventurous that it requires a personal attitude adjustment just to take it. This river rafting article represents travel adventure written as a personal experience.

Tapping your experience data bank: I have had quite a bit of experience here. I've been down the Colorado River on a raft, written a book about a lady who pioneered river rafting, hiked a lot, and know something about unusual action adventures.

Possible spin-offs: Let's explore the travel adventure angle. To appeal to this magazine, the topic must be something that seniors can do. This might suggest an educational field trip to excavate a ruin, an Outward Bound program for senior citizens, or a trailer caravan to Mexico that you can join. Offhand I can't think of any personal experience I've had (except the Colorado River trip) that would qualify here. If I had experienced any of these, I would have a possible travel adventure piece for this magazine.

I might be able to research one or all of these and prepare the piece as a roundup. Many universities now offer educational field trips that seniors can take. These vary from studying the ecology of an area to excavating Indian ruins in Arizona. This might appeal to seniors.

Article 4. "Do Grandparents Have Visitation Rights?" This article shows how grandparents learn to fight for rights to their grandchildren when there is a divorce.

Tapping your experience data bank: I don't know too much about this, but I like the subject and could have written it with a little research.

Possible spin-offs: Unfortunately, this piece does not suggest other articles to me.

Article 5. "Death Valley Awakens." A barren desert explodes with vibrant color: Death Valley in spring. This article features twelve color pictures of the flowers and scenery of the area. Generally it is a travel piece, almost a picture story. It explores a well-known area from a particular point of view: coming alive in the spring.

Tapping your experience data bank: I have a degree in biology and know something about plant life and the desert. I have done a lot of hiking in and around the desert and mountains, and I like this subject. I also have a file on national parks and other special places. As a result I could have written this piece easily.

Possible spin-offs: In trying to create similar articles the editor might like, I would start with other well-known places, probably national parks or monuments. In this case, the first place that comes to my mind is Mount Rainier National Park.

I have spent some time here and am really impressed with the floral beauty in midsummer just as the snow recedes. This would satisfy the need for a special angle, and would make a terrific picture story.

The second possibility the Death Valley piece suggests to me is Yosemite National Park. You could do something similar since Yosemite comes alive in the spring when the waterfalls are at their thundering best.

Another similar angle could be Yosemite in the fall when the animals are getting ready for winter, the valley is ablaze with color and the days have a very special feeling. By combining these angles with the sights to see, you could literally parallel the construction of the Death Valley article.

Article 6. "Unleashing the Furies." It's often better to express rather than suppress anger—even on the job. This article might be classified as personal psychology.

Tapping your experience data bank: I have clipping files on tension, anger, stress, and a number of similar subjects. This article could probably have been written out of my files. I also have quite a bit of information on the Phillip Zimbardo research about shyness.

Possible spin-offs: For me, this piece suggests articles on parallel subjects—tension, stress, shyness, jealousy, impatience, and other emotions that help or hinder individual performance.

Article 7. "How I Learned to Stop Worrying and Love the Swamp." The magazine invites readers to "join our adventurer on a journey above and below the waterline for an eyewitness account of the flora and fauna of the swamp he calls his own."

This is a nature article, literally a minicourse on swamp ecology that explains why we're losing the swamps, the benefits of a swamp, and which living things exist there.

Tapping your experience data bank: This is getting a little far afield for me.

Possible spin-offs: Any nature minicourse would fit here: sand dunes, beaches, marshes, meadows, alpine country, a mountain stream, a river, and tide pools.

If you decide that an article on a stream might be interesting to the magazine, the angle would probably be how some of the streams are being lost, what creatures live in a stream, and how to save them . . . basically a minicourse on stream ecology. The minicourses offered by this magazine include much more than nature. A recent one examined the Constitution. I would need to look at five to ten of these, however, to project out beyond the subject of nature.

Article 8. "Spokesman for Civil Rights." John Hope Franklin offers historical perspective. This is a personality piece about a distinguished black civil rights spokesman.

Tapping your experience data bank: Although I have written personality pieces, I would have to pass here.

Possible spin-offs: To parallel this, you would need something on seniors who have made a significant contribution. This might be a photographer who creates his own world, a senior who runs an organization to provide housing for the homeless, or a prominent, national figure.

Article 9. "Come On In, the Wine's Fine!" An Aromatic Guide for the Tasteful Traveler." This article explains how to taste wines and where the major wine areas are.

Tapping your experience data bank: I know absolutely nothing about wine except what I like, and I couldn't do the article. I have written a number of travel roundups and could probably suggest one of these. The problem is I don't understand how this particular article fits the magazine's scheme. Therefore, I would have a hard time suggesting parallel articles.

Possible spin-offs: This is partially a travel roundup, but it doesn't trigger much for me. I might try a roundup on winter carnivals, but the connection isn't clear.

The question that arises in my mind is whether the editor wants general travel roundups, or do roundups have to be connected to food in some way? Even if you're not really sure, always try.

Article 10. "The Choice Is Yours: Creating the Right Party Flavor." Cheeses, dips, fresh fruits, etc.—the article is complete with recipes.

Tapping your experience data bank: This is a good article, but not for me. I know nothing about food nor how to fix it.

Possible spin-offs: The angle here has to do with entertaining. I might suggest articles on backyard barbecuing, or picnic fixings.

Article 11. "Vacationing on the Railroad: How to Get the Most—Mileage and Comfort—from Your Train Pass." Train travel in Europe. This is European travel.

Tapping your experience data bank: This is the kind of article I could probably do. I have written a lot of travel articles, and this one appeals to me. But the European angle would be difficult. I would pass on this. It would be a better subject for someone who has been to Europe a few times. I don't consider this category to be train travel but foreign vacation travel. Foreign travel, especially European travel, is of special interest to this fairly affluent, older audience. Another title recently published in this series is: "A stroll in the Black Forest—Walk Through Germany's Deep Woods and Visit a World in a Time Capsule."

Possible spin-offs: Bed and breakfast places throughout Europe or trailering through France.

Article 12. "On the Town with a Senior Single: The Social Scene Can Be Fun for the Creative Person." This article stresses that senior singlehood is a wondrous thing. This piece addresses the social concerns of the senior.

Tapping your experience data bank: I don't know very much

about the seniors' social scene, but I'm sympathetic to it. I also have some knowledge of the social concerns of seniors and might be able to address some of them.

Possible spin-offs: Actually this magazine could easily run an article an issue on the "senior single." This particular piece, however, is fairly general, so I have to assume the common denominator here is social problems or social concerns that affect seniors. Possible articles in this vein might include getting acquainted in a new town and whether to move near the children.

That's six possible ideas, targeted to *this* magazine, generated by study of just one issue.

ANALYSIS OF MAGAZINE TWO   *Family Circle* is, of course, a service magazine for women. It generally publishes articles in these categories (they do not match exactly the *Family Circle* table of contents): food and nutrition, parenting and kids, your looks, money management and finance, your home, health and fitness, smart shopping/smart consumer, family/marriage problems, careers/jobs and work, your problems, antiques/crafts, true life and true drama, women's well-being/women's concerns, improving your life as a woman, celebrity profiles, current events, your auto, and a few other categories.

As I mentioned earlier, they also do crossovers. That is, they include short articles from several categories under blanket titles such as "The Cold Weather Survival Guide." Under this section they cover such topics as "Winterize your Health" and "Cold Weather Beauty."

The following articles appeared in the magazine over several months:

Article 1.   "Thirty Days to a Better Job." This article tells how readers can make more money at more satisfying jobs by following a four-week plan. It is for the working women in the readership.

Tapping your experience data bank: I have spent some time putting together resumes, read several books on the subject and know several ways to write resumes. I have a lot of information on how to make yourself more valuable to your employer. I have also been clipping everything I could find about jobs and work from the newspaper and have a number of ideas about creating your own job and other things. From this material I could obviously create work and work-related articles with different angles.

Possible spin-offs: The angle here seems to be making more money for women, so let's try to come up with some related titles that do this. Here are a couple I can think of: "Six High Paying Careers That Take Little Training" and "How to Make Your Current Job Pay Top Dollar."

Article 2.   "Winning Window Gardens." Now you can have a garden without having a yard! All it takes is a window (in sun or shade), a few plants and a window box.

Tapping your experience data bank: I have been a gardener for years, have written a number of garden articles, and several garden books. I know gardening backwards and forwards and have a gardening library. Obviously I have enough material in my data bank to let me do any number of gardening articles.

Possible spin-offs: This has to do with gardening without a yard or gardening in small spaces. While this magazine takes a wider range of garden articles than this, they might well take some more within this scope. These could include "Big Color in Small Spaces," "Window Salad Gardens," and "Growing Tomatoes Indoors at Christmas." I sold the latter one to *Family Circle,* with a list of tomato varieties that can be grown indoors in small containers.

Article 3.   "Five Ways to Prevent Teen Pregnancy." Each year a million girls get pregnant, many of them little more than babies themselves. How can we prevent this tragedy? Here are some promising answers.

Tapping your experience data bank: I haven't put together a file on teen problems. I personally don't feel in touch with teens. And I don't really want to write an article, any article, on this subject.

Possible spin-offs: Some of the problems that parents have, of course, are teenage driving and alcohol, and teen suicide.

Article 4.   "You Need a Tune Up, Lady! How to get what you pay for." The teaser line says, "When your car needs tuning, do you leave it with a mechanic and simply hope for the best? Don't! Use these expert tips to get the right service and proper work for your money."

The category, of course, is automobiles, including service, repair and related subjects handled from a woman's point of view.

Tapping your experience data bank: I am all thumbs when it comes to cars. But I do understand the problem that women have trying to deal with automotive problems. In addition I once owned a tire store, and understand tires, front end alignment and brake repair.

Possible spin-offs: I would consider other automotive related problems that women have trouble with. How about buying tires? Few men, and even fewer women, know much about this subject. And it does need clarification. In addition there are problems women run into trying to buy a used car, and a new car. These are possibilities.

I could have written three out of four: a respectable batting average in any league. The more issues of a magazine that you survey, of course, the more article ideas you will be able to come up with.

MAKE A LIST   After you have developed a number of possible spinoffs for the magazine you have surveyed, go back through and make a list of the ones you would actually like to try. From the list that I generated for *Modern Maturity,* I would seriously like to try "The Summer Gardens of Mount Rainier," "Yosemite Bursts into Spring," "Shyness Affects Us All," and "Minicourse: the Ecology of a Mountain Stream." The one I would try first would be the piece on Yosemite.

For *Family Circle,* I would probably try the piece on tires, slanted about the same way as the tune-up piece.

DO THE BASIC RESEARCH   Now do enough additional research to allow you to write a query for each article you decide to try. On the Yosemite article, I probably have enough in the files to write the query easily. Later on I'll need to request the pictures from either the Park Service or the company that runs the park lodges.

For the article on shyness, I probably have enough material in the files. I will also need to do a little thinking about how shyness affects each individual. When I put these thoughts together I'm ready to write the query.

WRITE YOUR QUERY   Now, actually write the query (see page 117 for a complete discussion of how to write a good query letter). Do the best job you can, taking into account the magazine's style, focus, and readership.

If that query comes back, go to the next one. A given idea may not sell for a variety of reasons. After all, you are only making an educated guess. The first couple of times you work with a magazine you might not hit the mark, but keep trying.

FIVE TIPS FOR CREATING TOP-NOTCH IDEAS FROM INDIVIDUAL MAGAZINES

I know from experience that this system works well. Over the years I have sold hundreds of articles by letting the magazine generate the idea as we have just done in this chapter. The method works for every magazine, but don't expect to create the same number of ideas with each publication. Sometimes when I thumb through a periodical I am lucky to turn up one possible idea, whereas other times I come away with dozens. Here are some tips that will help make the system work for you.

1. *Practice, practice, practice.* Most writers are so used to creating the idea first that many have difficulty starting with the magazine. The secret is practice. Immerse yourself in the idea. Thumb through as many publications as possible and try creating ideas for every title.

Go through the same magazine several times; put it away for a while, and then take it out and try again. Also look at as many different magazines as possible. After a while you will discover that letting the magazine suggest the idea will become almost second nature and that you will start coming up with possible ideas the minute you see the titles on the cover.

2. *Concentrate on your favorite subjects.* In explaining the system here, I have tried to create an idea from every title. It doesn't work that way in practice. You will generate far more and better ideas if you skip the subjects that don't interest you and concentrate on areas that have appeal. That article on cars in a publication might well turn you off, but that piece on a widow who restores Victorian houses might just create a spark.

Those occasional "sparks" are the things that make good salable ideas.

3. *When you're on a roll, keep creating.* Sometimes you'll discover that some word or phrase in a title will touch a creative chord, and you will come up with half a dozen ideas almost effortlessly. When this happens, don't cut yourself off. Let the ideas flow until they run out. In some cases, I've been able to create fifteen to twenty viable ideas this way. On a flight to Los Angeles several years ago, I happened to glance at an article in *Western's World* about a woman who retired to Mexico, built her own adobe house, and opened a now-famous cooking school. This article triggered my memory of older women who had made some unusual contribution. I was so excited that I worked on this until the plane landed. The result was six articles I wouldn't have written otherwise.

4. *Create the best possible title.* There are a lot of different kinds of titles. Generally titles ask a question ("Do you own a gold mine in gold jewelry?"), use direct address ("Grow Your Own Salad"), offer a promise ("Squeezing the Most Out of a Lemon"), state exactly what the subject is ("Helping an Unpopular Child"), and may include catch phrases or word combinations that attract attention ("Glitter Glamor"). Many titles also use selling words: *quick, best, miracle, great,* and *super* ("Super Easy Ices"). Titles are often changed by the editor, but since they help sell an article originally, you should always create the best possible "selling" title for every article you write.

In addition, when you generate possible titles from existing article titles, it helps to parallel the titles of the magazine you're examining. That is, make yours have the same slant. Editors often have a preference for particular types of titles. Your idea may come out "How to Get a Raise" but the magazine uses titles that offer a promise such as "Great Ways to Earn $25,000 or More." So take a hint, and jazz up your title the same way. A possibility might be: "Ten Ways to Make Your Boss Say Yes: How to Ask for a Raise and Get It."

5. *Ask yourself questions.* If you look through a magazine and go blank, try asking yourself questions about the titles. For instance, if one of the titles was "If Not Satisfied, Get Your Mon-

ey Back or More: You Don't Have to Put Up With Poorly Made Products," I might ask, "How do I get satisfaction if my car is a lemon? What happens if a contractor I've hired does a poor job? What if someone overcharges me at a store and I don't realize it until I get home? What if someone sends me a letter and it doesn't arrive? Can I take action against the post office? What do I do if my supermarket continually sells poor produce?" I could go on and on, but with a little effort I can probably expand each one of those questions into a possible article.

CREATE SIMILAR, NOT IDENTICAL, IDEAS   If a magazine has an article on how to save money shopping warehouse stores, you wouldn't want to duplicate this idea. That particular magazine wouldn't be interested. But the theme here is saving money and the magazine might be interested in other ways their readers can save money shopping. So you suggest to the same magazine an article titled "How to Save Money through Discount Catalogs." It's a completely different idea, but it has many of the same elements.

Here are some guidelines:

1. Look for the common denominator in every article idea.

2. Try to come up with specific article ideas within that common denominator that the same magazine might like.

3. Query the magazine you have surveyed about the best of the ideas you've generated.

REWORKING THE SAME IDEA   Can you ever take a magazine's idea, rework the same concept and resell it? Of course you can, but not to that magazine. If you think warehouse shopping is a good idea, you might use the original article as a research source, do more research on your own, and write a warehouse shopping article you would sell to another magazine. If I found the idea in a women's magazine, for instance, I might try a short piece on this subject for a hunting and fishing magazine, concentrating on how to shop for firearms, fishing tackle, and similar merchandise. Or I might sell the same general concept to an automotive magazine. Ideas cannot be copyrighted, and you're welcome to use them all as long as you use only the facts and add your own angles and point of view.

SPINNING OFF OVER AND OVER

Don't stop when you sell that first article. As before, the initial sale is just the beginning. The next step is to take this article and, using the methods explained in chapter 2, spin your idea off into ideas for as many other magazines as possible.

Now you have two basic methods for selling articles fairly easily. You can either start with the idea and, using one of the systems from chapter 2, come up with possible markets. Or you can start with the market and come up with an idea that an editor is likely to buy. In practice, you should work both ways so that you create ideas for the magazines you would like to write for and at the same time make a number of sales from each of your article ideas.

4. How to Establish Yourself with Editors

Actually it's easy to establish yourself with an editor so that he or she will buy your articles regularly, will sometimes call you for assignments, and will often depend on you to provide the magazine with certain types of articles.

I have a friend who sold an article to *Omni* magazine because an *Omni* editor saw one of his articles in another publication, liked his writing style and gave him an assignment. This first sale was followed by a number of others.

At first, this writer simply contributed pieces for some of the continuing features and columns carried by the magazine. Then his editor was assigned to cover outer space for the magazine.

The writer knew almost nothing about the subject. But the editor asked him to handle assignments on outer space because he, the editor, had confidence in this author's writing. Last time I talked to the writer, he had just come back from an assignment to cover a space station convention in Boulder, Colorado. He was learning about space, fast, and having a great time handling the assignments.

In my own case, I had worked for *Trailer Life* magazine for about five years. At the time I had a column running in the magazine and also sold them about an article a month. One morning I received a call from the editor/publisher who asked what I knew about boating. My answer was "nothing." "Fine," he said,

"You're going to be our field editor for a new magazine called *Family Houseboating*."

The next few years, I flew around the country testing houseboats for the magazine. Although I didn't know much about houseboats when I started, I knew a great deal by the time I finished.

FOLLOW THAT FIRST SALE IMMEDIATELY

In trying to establish yourself with an individual editor, the place to start is with an initial sale of one article. But remember, that's just the beginning.

Follow that first sale with another query and sale almost immediately. Your new idea must be of real interest to the editor, as explained in chapter 2, but write that next query within a few weeks of the first acceptance.

As soon as the second article has been sold, put your next idea on the editor's desk. By the time you have made six or seven sales, you will have begun to establish a relationship with that editor. And that is the secret to selling a continuous series of articles to any one magazine.

ALMOST STAFF

Your object is to try to work almost as staff on one magazine. This frequently happens when an editor knows your work is professional and starts to rely on you for certain types of coverage.

In one case, with a retirement magazine, I started out with an article on trailering for retirees, came back with a piece on a couple who lived in a mobile home, and then did another on mobile home park living.

Somehow that made me an expert on recreational vehicles and mobile homes. After that, over the next four years, the editor assigned me to handle every piece on the subject that appeared in the magazine. I wrote a complete supplement on mobile home living, a long article on how to buy a trailer, a piece on full-time trailering, and a lot more.

With *Western Outfitter*, I began by compiling a retail roundup piece over the phone. The editor Anne DeReuter liked this article so well, she asked for another, then another until I was writing all their merchandising articles every month.

CORE INCOME

The first step is to establish yourself with one magazine. The second is to cultivate another magazine the minute that first publication purchases articles from you on a regular basis. Continue until six or seven publications accept your material every month or every few months. You now have created what I call your "core income." This gives you a base income each month with which to pay the bills.

After that, if you have extra time, you can work on columns, try to hit the bigger magazines, explore some writing project you've had to put off, or even write a book.

SUGGEST IDEAS REGULARLY   In the writing business, you'll find that the more ideas you suggest to magazines, the more go-aheads you'll get. And as the editor begins to know your work, you'll also start receiving assignments you didn't solicit.

In one instance, Scripps Howard Business Publications, on the basis of one idea, suddenly began to assign me two or three articles a month. This went on for two years, all because I suggested one idea the editor really liked. These ideas should generally be suggested using the query format. You will find a complete discussion of queries on page 117. Sometimes you can suggest an idea in a phone conversation, once you and an editor have gotten acquainted, but often the editor will also want to see it in writing.

Editors don't know what they want until you show them. This statement is mostly true, but not quite. Often an editor and a magazine will project a general editorial direction, but not a specific one. A retirement magazine will decide to run articles on mobile home living, or they will decide to expand their coverage to include travel and retirement areas around the country.

In many cases, they don't know which specific articles they need until they see them. This means that if you propose a well-written article that fits the general plan, most editors will buy it or assign you to do it.

Recently I suggested a yearly economic forecast article to a number of my retail trade business editors. Several wrote back and said, "We hadn't thought about doing a forecast, but it's a great idea that's important to our readers." As a result, I sold these forecasts to *Garden Supply Retailer, Yarn Market News, Photographic Trade News,* and a number of others. This year, I forgot about the article until I received letters from two of the editors saying, "We want to run that forecast piece again."

Cultivate a reputation for knowing what particular editors need. Editors like to deal with freelancers who understand a magazine's needs. How do you do this? You start by reading the magazine from cover to cover as we did in chapter 1. But that's just the beginning.

After you have sold a few articles to a magazine and have begun to build a relationship with one particular editor, ask that editor to put you on the mailing list (many magazines will do this to make sure their regular contributors keep up with what they are publishing). As each new issue comes in, go over every article carefully and ask yourself, Why was this included? How does it help this magazine's readers? If I were the editor, what other subjects would I cover in the next issue? What would I be running six months from now?

After awhile, you'll start to get a sixth sense about the magazine. And in many cases you'll begin to understand it as well as the editor does.

SUGGEST SIMILAR ARTICLES The next step is to suggest articles that show you can provide the type of material this publication wants. A good way to do this is to pick out a series of articles the magazine is running and offer two or three more pieces that will either fit the series or complement it.

A woman's magazine, for instance, might be stressing jobs and work. That might lead me to suggest that women in the workplace are just as interested in part-time or temporary work as they are in full-time employment, or that their readers might like one or several articles on home businesses. However, I wouldn't be nearly as general as this; I would offer specific ideas with a twist.

Once I have sold a magazine several articles and the editor has seen that I have a clear idea of what the publication wants, he or she will often call and ask me to come up with additional material in other areas.

Recently I received a request from a trade journal for Christmas merchandising ideas. "Could you," the editor asked, "submit twelve possible article ideas along this line?" Another magazine relied on me over several years to generate all the articles they ran on retirees. All of this was made possible because I demonstrated that I knew the magazine well and turned out articles they could use.

Become super-familiar with a magazine's article format and style.   Before you send off any article, make sure it is written in the same style and format as similar articles in the publication. This will help establish you as a writer who pays close attention to the magazine's needs. Fail to do this and, although you may make some sales, you will eventually lose out to the competition.

This was brought home to me emphatically several years ago when one of my writing friends received a go-ahead from *Cosmopolitan* magazine. The kicker in his query about CB radios had been that "they're also a great way to meet men." The letter asking for the article, signed by Helen Gurley Brown, came within five days after *Cosmo* had received the query.

This writer then wrote the article adding a lot of technical information on the frequencies and how CBs worked. I kept telling her that this just didn't match the magazine's style. She ignored me. When she finished she mailed it in, expecting a check. The reply came within seven days: "Too technical for us! Try *Popular Mechanics!*"

What this writer overlooked was that each magazine and each editor has a way of doing things and a style that come through in every article.

One publication I used to work for always used quite a few statistics, five to six anecdotes, and two or three quotes in every article. The rest of the piece contained about forty percent facts, explanation with examples, and the opinion of the writer. Articles that didn't come close to matching this were rejected.

The article format checklist.   Here is a method I use frequently to find the pattern a particular magazine uses. Use this checklist to analyze the published articles in the magazine or magazines you wish to write for.

- Start by deciding on the viewpoint. Is this article written in the first person (I or we), second person (you), or third person (he, she, they)? Does the article speak directly to the reader as "you"?

- Consider the types of leads used. Leads found most frequently in articles are the anecdote, quote, striking or provocative statement, question, straight declarative summation, summation, and statistical leads. I will include examples here so you can easily classify the leads for yourself.

Anecdotal lead. Article title: "Courage Is Where You Find It." Lead: Jane Ralston did not hear the deep "beep-beep" of the logging truck's horn as the truck, brakes gone, thundered down on her from behind. At that moment she was concentrating too hard on the job of negotiating the school bus, with its 16 passengers, down the narrow winding mountain road. Neither did she hear the near hysterical shouts of the children as they frantically tried to get her attention.

For her, the first hint of danger came when the truck hit the rear of the bus with a sickening crash and sent it bouncing like a toy toward the cliff.

"Suddenly the steering wheel wouldn't work," she recollects. "All I could see was sky, then the river almost 400 feet below. I screamed, threw my hands in front of my face, and prayed. I was absolutely positive that within minutes we would all be dead."

Provocative statement. Article title: "Country Living Isn't What It Used To Be." Lead: Going away and leaving the doors unlocked has always been one of the real pleasures of living in the country. But a growing number of rural residents are returning home to find their homes burgled. And in a few communities such as Montmorenci, Indiana, rural thieves driving a moving van now systematically raid local farms, making off with everything from the furniture to the family cow.

Question. Article title: "When You Attend a Boarding School." Lead: What is life really like in a boarding school when you're fourteen and wish you were still living at home?

Straight declarative. Article title: "The Recreational Heritage of Our National Parks." Lead: Our national parks represent one of the best recreational values around anywhere today. The possibilities range from rock climbing, to glacier scrambling and scuba diving, to camping out in a desert several hundred feet below sea level. The fact is that no matter what your pleasure, you'll be able to engage in that activity in at least one national park.

Quote. Article title: "Oh, Those Hardworking Oldsters." Lead: When conference director George Haines went to work for the state of New York back in 1930, he considered what he was doing to be just a job. "Today," he says, "It's my whole life. And although I am now long past retirement age, I fully expect to die with my 'work boots' on.' "

Summation. Article title: "The Gourmet Department Store." Lead: If you live in New York City and are looking for a serious source of fine foods from all over the world, you'd do well to take a closer look at Bloomingdale's. Here Petrossians offers the best caviar and smoked salmon in New York. And across the aisle, Compotoir Gourmand sells gourmet dishes freshly prepared by several well known French chefs. In addition, Marcella Hazan, author of the "Classic Italian Cookbook" has developed a line of high-quality Italian goods for Bloomingdale's including extra-virgin, cold-pressed olive oils. Besides this, the store offers a cheese cellar, a Southwest section, and a bakery strong on American classics including some of the best brownies in the city and excellent Bundt cakes.

Statistical. Article title: "So You Want To Move To The Country." Lead: America is on the move again and this time it's back to the country in droves! Believe it or not, last year 400,000 people moved from the city to rural America in what has been dubbed as the great middle class "back to the land movement" of the 80's.

Historically, the U.S. population has migrated from agricultural areas to urban centers. But now in a startling turn-around, rural areas everywhere are growing at a fantastic rate. While the five biggest cities in the United States dropped 5 percent between 1970 and 1977, the rural counties grew by an estimated 11 percent.

- Underline the *capsule sentence*. This sentence states the theme the article intends to prove and is generally located just after the lead. Ask yourself, does this statement come in the first paragraph, the second, or where? Here are capsule sentences for some of the above leads:

Article title: "Courage Is Where You Find It." Capsule sentence: Jane at that time had been driving for only a year. But when the regular bus driver failed to show up at the end of the day, she had reluctantly agreed to drive the children home from the school picnic (now you are going on to describe the adventure).

Article title: "Country Living Is Not What It Used To Be." Capsule sentence: (second paragraph) Without a doubt rural crime today is becoming a real problem.

Article title: "When You Attend a Boarding School." Capsule sentence: (second paragraph) The answer is that sometimes it can be a lot of fun, at other times, a bit lonely.

Article title: "The Recreational Heritage of Our National Parks." Capsule sentence: (first paragraph) The fact is that no matter what your pleasure you'll be able to engage in that activity in at least one national park.

- Pick out the anecdotes, quotes, statistics and dialogue (two people speaking to each other). Mark these with an "A", a "Q", an "S", or a "D" at the immediate right of each paragraph in which they appear.

- What kind of authorities are used? Some magazines let you use general authorities such as a leading merchandising expert, a leading psychologist or whatever. Others demand you name national authorities, the institution at which the person works, and the city in which they're located. Still others will sometimes let you get away with very informal authorities such as "the old ranger."

- Underline the negative phrases that contain words like "don't," "none," "not," and similar words. You'll find that most magazines keep these "negatives" to a minimum. Some don't tolerate any, or they tolerate very few. As a general rule, try to state most things in a positive way. Instead of saying, "Don't leave the drawers open," you should say, "close the drawers."

- Underline all exposition (background information) and explanations. Put an E beside the paragraphs that contain these. Count them, and then compare the total to the total number of paragraphs in the article to get an idea of how much exposition/explanation the magazine prefers.

- How does the article end? Does the ending tie into the lead? Does it leave the reader with a satisfied feeling? Does it use a question, a summary, a quote, or what?

- Are the articles talky? Formal? Informal? Flamboyant? Are the sentences long, complex, and packed with information? Or are they short and conversational?

When you finish the first draft of your article, mark it up the same way we did the magazine's article. You will now be able to see at a glance if you have followed the magazine's format. If your article's style doesn't match the magazine's in most respects, change your piece so that it does.

You may have to analyze several articles from a particular publication before you begin to understand the pattern. You should, of course, expect both the pattern and style to change whenever a new editor takes over the magazine. I discover this by watching the masthead carefully. It is the only reliable way I know to obtain this information close to the time it happens.

If you study markets this way and have ideas suitable to the publication, you will often sell the first time and build a solid, continuing acceptance for your material from the editor.

ACT ON WHAT EDITORS SAY THEY ARE DOING

In a recent issue of *Modern Maturity,* editor Robert Wood told about an expansion in current events coverage. "This change," he says in an editorial, "reflects the drive of the magazine to bring readers more information on developments affecting each of us as consumers, voters, and activists." Checking the magazine itself, you see articles on savings bonds (personal finance), the outlook for peace (international affairs), and problems affecting seniors.

Wood also stated that the magazine is going to do more of this. That means, since the program just started, they are probably looking for more articles in this vein. If you write this kind of article, by all means query immediately.

ACT ON THE READERS' CONCERNS

In the same issue of *Modern Maturity,* a reader gripes about how snowmobiles are causing significant environmental damage. Maybe the editor would be willing to explore this subject from the standpoint of an environmentalist's concern.

Another letter talks about an article on the phone company, saying we should let AT&T take over the post office. This might trigger an article on private mail services—how efficient they are and how well they do.

A letter in *Friendly Exchange,* the Farmer's Insurance Company magazine, talks about children's reactions in a fire—the fear they can experience and how some children hide in a closet before attempting to escape from the fire. This might trigger an article on children's reactions to other emergencies. Another letter talks about the liability insurance concerns in response to an editorial. Again this could trigger several articles on why court awards are so high and what we can do about it.

CONTINUALLY OFFER NEW TWISTS

Articles in writers' magazines sometimes quote editors as saying, "Give me something different." Invariably writers misinterpret the word *different,* and begin coming up with ideas that don't fit the magazine at all. A magazine that takes only non-fiction will suddenly begin receiving fiction and poetry. Or a magazine that buys only technical automotive articles will be sent a piece on how to buy a car.

This isn't what the editors want at all. What they are saying is, "Give me a twist or a new way of looking at the subjects we are already covering."

THE TWIST DEFINED Just what is a twist? Let's define it for our purposes as "the unusual in a usual situation." What is that? Well, most people raise pets. The usual pet is a dog, cat, turtle, fish, bird, or hamster. The unusual is an alligator, an ostrich, or an elephant. If a magazine regularly ran stories on pet owners and their pets, the unusual or a twist to this would be a piece on three children who owned a pet elephant.

LOOK FOR WHAT'S DIFFERENT   Let's try again. A lot of people travel in recreational vehicles. Most of these vehicles are standard makes of trailers, motor homes, and camper coaches. But what if someone bought an old airplane, put four wheels on the body and turned it into a nice-looking luxury trailer? That's different, and that's a twist. It is also a topic I've seen several published articles about in the trailer magazines.

These same trailer magazines also frequently run articles on people who trailer full-time. Most of these are standard. But what if we find a retiree who trailers full-time by himself and goes around the country doing good deeds for poor families? Now, we have a twist that makes the piece extraordinary.

KEEP PRACTICING   If you want to become good at this, I suggest you practice taking some common subjects and ask yourself, "What's different?" Let's try this with a couple of subjects and see how it works.

Schools.   A lot of articles are written on such subjects as how to help your child do better in school, how to rate your child's teacher, and should sex education be taught. These are good topics, but more or less standard fare.

Now, what would be different? Some of the things I can think of quickly are: conducting regular school outdoors, letting the kids grade themselves, conducting public school like a private school, and running a school without teachers. All of these are rather incongruous with the conventional idea of a school.

Recently I discovered one of these topics used in *Family Circle Magazine* with the title, "How To Get Your Child a 'Private School Education' in a Public School." This is an idea with a twist that satisfies the editor's and the magazine's desire for something different.

Jobs.   Because of the current interest, a number of magazines regularly run articles on jobs. Here are a few possibilities that have a twist: "Jobs You Can Do at Home," "Jobs That Let You Travel the World," and "Jobs That Are More Play than Work."

I frequently find twists like these in *Family Circle*. A recent one was "How to Get Part-Time Jobs That Earn Big Bucks." This is a roundup of part-time jobs that require minimum training, pay well, and let you set your own schedule.

This is different because normally you would expect part-time jobs to pay fairly low wages.

Money. Different approaches could be: living the good life without money, banking in Europe from your hometown, friends and your money. As mentioned, *Family Circle* recently published a piece entitled "How Not To Lose Friends Over Money," which detailed ten incidents that can create money problems with friends.

While some of the twists given here have sold, that doesn't mean they are dead as article ideas. The basic idea of how not to lose friends over money can probably be sold to other magazines right now. You of course can't sell a *Family Circle* article written by someone else, but you can take the idea, research it yourself, and put the idea into your own words, using new quotes, anecdotes, and statistics. Also, by changing the angle slightly you may be able to sell something similar to *Family Circle* again in a few years. What you sell will be an entirely different article using a slightly different theme, maybe: "Don't Let Money Come Between You and Your Friends."

Now, try this yourself. Do it just as we did here. Start with a subject and try to come up with as many different angles as you can think of. When you have created five or ten good angles, pick the best ones to develop into full articles.

STAY AHEAD OF THE TIMES   Many magazines today like to keep up with the latest developments in whatever field they report on. For these magazines, you need to be on the lookout for the latest in medical advances, the newest fads, developing problems that haven't quite surfaced yet, and anything else the magazine covers that could be considered new.

I know several writers who do a superior job at this. One clipped six or seven newspapers every day looking for anything new. One day, she noticed a small item in the local paper about a new program to help underachieving students by taking them directly into the labs of large companies like IBM. Here they were exposed to the latest in scientific research. This exposure revolutionized the lives of a number of them.

The article this lady wrote sold to a number of publications and generated several assignments. Over the years she has stayed on the leading edge of developments in her field and, as a result, has become a regular contributor to a number of major magazines.

ALWAYS GIVE THE EDITOR SOMETHING EXTRA

An editor of mine once said what readers want most is "take home" value, and that's true. As a result, an editor will love you if you offer the reader extra value in every article. How do you do this? Three ways:

OFFER EXTRA DETAIL   The more detail you put in an article, up to the point of saturation, the better an editor and the reader will like it. In a travel article, a reader wants to know what the trip costs, what to see, where to stay or camp, the distances between major points, even what they'll find on the breakfast menu. Readers want a clear picture of whatever you're writing about.

Details make the difference.   Even in a personality piece, the reader wants all the little peculiarities that make an individual interesting. One short *Reader's Digest* piece on an unusual builder detailed the clothes he wore, his habits (such as crawling under buildings with a flashlight in his mouth), his verbal expressions, and all of this unusual man's idiosyncrasies.

An editor likes it when the writer goes that extra mile and digs out colorful extras that make a story interesting. When you consistently do this, the editor is more likely to give you a go-ahead on that next article than he would if you simply turned in a minimum effort.

OFFER THE READERS STEPS TO POSITIVE ACTION   Years ago another editor told me "If you want to give your reader 'take home value' and make an editor love you, offer *steps to positive action*." That is, if you tell the reader to do something, you must also detail exactly what steps he must take to do it.

If you ask that reader to homestead his property, you must explain, in steps, what forms he needs and where to get them, how to fill out those forms, where to take them within the county to file, and what to expect when he gets there.

Here is a sample of how to do this from a *Family Circle* article, "Social Drinking: How to Play It Safe," which was reprinted in the magazine from the book *How to Cut Down on Your Social Drinking* by Richard A. Basini (G.P. Putnam's Sons).

The instructions are written to the hostess about how to keep her guests from getting pie-eyed at a dinner party. I will just list the subtitles here, but you get the point. Each of those subtitles is discussed in the text with a short paragraph or two.

- Don't Invite Problems
- Offer Plenty of Food
- Serve Dinner Promptly
- Refrain from Refilling
- Avoid the Nightcap Trap
- Do It the French Way (Serve Sparkling Mineral Water)
- Put Away the Bottles
- Feature the Juice, Not the Booze

In writing steps, always start with a verb, as the author did here so you are giving instructions: offer, serve, refrain, avoid, do, put away, and feature. Don't start these with a preposition or adverb, as some writers are prone to do. Examples:

Right: Put away the bottles.

Wrong: To discourage having a drink after dinner, put away the bottles.

Right: Refrain from refilling.

Wrong: At a party, don't run to refill the minute guests empty their glasses.

Right: Don't offer additional drinks at the end of the evening.

Wrong: At the end of the evening you should refrain from offering additional drinks.

INCLUDE SIDEBARS WHENEVER POSSIBLE   The more information you can give the reader, the more valuable your article will be. I generally take a look at my article and try to see if that piece might lend itself to "sidebar" information. A sidebar is simply material that is not included in the body of the article, but is enclosed in a box at the bottom or side of the page.

For a trade magazine in the lawn service field, I did a piece entitled, "Words of Wisdom for Direct Mail Advertising." It was designed to show lawn care entrepreneurs how to use direct mail. I wrote a fairly comprehensive article on direct mail, then added several special boxes that addressed specific subjects (see fig. 4-1). These consisted of a direct mail checklist, a box on overcoming skepticism, and a word power sidebar.

PICK A SPECIALTY

Magazines like to buy their articles from an expert. There are several reasons for this. First, magazines like to feel that their writers know what they're talking about. If you've written fifteen or twenty articles on the same subject, they're more likely to trust you as an authority in the field. In addition, if you've built your name as an expert, readers are likely to know your name and trust your opinion. This is important to a magazine.

WHAT SPECIALTIES ARE THERE?   There are many fields in which you can specialize. Let's look quickly at a few broad ones.

Business.   Just for starters there are over 4,000 business magazines that take articles in specialized business areas. They buy interviews with industry leaders, articles on business problems, general business areas, and more.

In addition, the popular magazines buy hundreds of business articles a year. Here are a few titles from the major women's magazines: "Credit-Crazed Dolls" (the credit situation), "Who's Afraid of the Big Bad Bank?" (a discussion of how to deal with a bank), "Birth of a Saleswoman" (an investigation of this glamorous, high paying field), "Career Power and How to Get It," and "Crash Course in Personal Finance." If you are business-minded, this can be a lucrative field.

Science.   There's hardly a field more in demand today than science. Pick up practically any magazine and you'll find an article on some aspect of science: agriculture, anthropology, astronomy, space, aviation, biology, chemistry, physics, zoology, and more.

The secret of breaking into this field is the same as it is for any other—study the magazines you're interested in hitting to determine what types of science articles they're taking. Use your local paper, as well as your local college public relations department, to

Word power

The words you choose to convey your message are important, so measure them carefully. Some of the best words and phrases are:

Free	Easy
New	You pay only...
At last	You'll be able to...
You	Two weeks from now you'll...
Only a few at this price...	Private invitation to...

WEAK WORDS	TRIGGER WORDS
Postage-PAID envelope.	Postage-FREE envelope.
We HIRED A DESIGNER.	We COMMISSIONED a designer.
A DOZEN.	A SET OF TWELVE.
This is your CHANCE. (50/50)	This is your OPPORTUNITY.
IF you decide to...	WHEN you decide to...
Take this TEST. (Sounds hard)	Take this QUIZ. (Sounds easy and fun.)
One of A handful...	One of THE handful...

Replace intellectual words with emotional words.

INTELLECTUAL WORD	EMOTIONAL WORD
Avid	Eager
Concerned	Worried
Construct	Build
Disclose	Explain
Experiment	Test
Immediately	Right now
Is provided with	Has
Learn	Find out
Observed	Seen
Preserve	Save
Select	Pick
Service	Take care of
Sufficient	Enough
Superior to	Better than
We would like to	We want to

Figure 4-1. Sidebars add additional useful information that doesn't fit within the article itself.

discover possible science articles on topics you'd like investigating and writing about.

Medicine.   In an increasing number of publications today, you'll find such articles as "What You Should Know About Male Cancers," "Do-It-Yourself Breast and Gynecological Checkup," and "New Ways to Cure Your Cancer." It isn't necessary to be a doctor to write articles like these, but you must do your homework well and build an extensive knowledge of this field.

Food/Nutrition.   Is this a good specialty? You bet it is. Of course, most food articles in the major magazines are staff written. You will, however, find freelance pieces like "Calorie Watch," "Cooking for Good Health: The Ten Star Vegetables," and "Watching Your Weight—How to Decalorize Your Favorite Recipes." There are also numerous secondary markets such as *Modern Maturity, Family Magazine, Earthtone, Grit, Woodmen of the World,* and *American Health,* which collectively buy hundreds of food and nutrition articles each year.

Building a specialty means accumulating a library of all possible markets. As a start, go through *Writer's Market* and send for every magazine that takes women's features—don't overlook the religious magazines, farm magazines, company magazines, health magazines, and others.

Automotive.   Pick up any popular magazine and you're liable to find at least one article on the car. In *Home Mechanix,* you'll find a number of specialized articles in each issue such as "Engine Oils and Additives: Truth and Friction" and "Why Car Repairs Cost So Much." Even in *Family Circle,* you'll find articles with titles like "You Need a Tune Up, Lady."

Follow the rule of collecting information, relating your own experiences to what's being done, and then querying.

Travel.   Everyone thinks they can write travel articles, but it's still a good specialty, as discussed in chapter 2. The market boils down to a limited number of travel magazines, travel sections in newspapers, and a much larger number of general and specialty magazines that take some travel articles.

To find these, start your own library of magazines that take travel articles—go through *Writer's Market* and send for copies. In addition, scan magazines you're not familiar with to see if they might be a market for one of your travel pieces.

Outdoor Recreation. Outdoor recreation today has exploded in many directions: recreation vehicles, boating, camping, hunting and fishing, water skiing, archery, skiing, snowmobiling, canoeing, bicycling, river running, sailboarding, surfing, skin diving, and much more. You will find articles on these subjects in specialized publications like *RV Lifestyle Magazine, Cycling U.S.A., Bowhunter Magazine,* and *Rowing USA.* These articles are also included in conservation publications like *American Forests, Bird Watcher's Digest, High Country News,* and *National Parks.* You will also find hundreds of outdoor articles published every year in the general magazines.

Other specialties that get good receptions at magazines include fashions, marriage, the family and its problems, women's issues, Hollywood celebrities, politics, education, and religion.

MAKE YOURSELF A SPECIALIST

To start specializing, pick a field you like or that you have a feeling for. After that, follow these steps: (1) Go through *Writer's Market* and send for all possible magazines that might take articles you write. (2) Look up articles in your field in the *Reader's Guide to Periodical Literature* (available in the library) and study the magazines that publish these articles. (3) Start reading technical journals—if it's medicine you're interested in, take the AMA Journal and others. Do the same for other fields. Also make yourself aware of any indexes in your fields. Your librarian can help you with these.

After this, the rest is up to you. A writer doesn't have to know everything he or she is writing about, but you must go to somebody who does. The public relations office of every major university can provide you with a list of specialists at their university who will answer questions over the phone. Finally, you must continue to work in the field, build your files, collect voluminous literature on the subject, and read extensively.

USE SALESMANSHIP

Writers don't like to admit this, but the job of becoming a consistently selling writer is almost fifty percent sales and fifty percent writing. Some writers I know actually spend more of their time searching for ideas, writing queries, and following up than they do writing the articles.

Here are a few basic rules to help you become a good salesman or saleswoman.

Switch to first names as quickly as possible.   Even in my initial query to an editor I sign my first name. Then the minute he or she answers with their first name, I switch over. All correspondence from then on is on a first name basis.

Make some personal comments related to your project. Many writers in their initial cover letter simply say something like "Here's the article you asked for" and sign their name. The idea is that brevity gets the point across and saves both the time of the writer and the editor. And of course it does, but it doesn't set you apart as a personality who might be remembered.

It doesn't hurt, after you've told the editor that the article is enclosed, to make a statement that is related to the article, yet still offers some insight into your personality.

Erle Stanley Gardner, a master salesman as well as a prolific writer, always wrote rather talkative letters that showed off the Gardner personality. He did this, in most cases, by referring to something the editor was interested in.

I too use this technique as often as possible. For instance, I have one editor who recently moved her office to Atlanta. I had been to Atlanta once to do a TV appearance. On this particular program I had to follow a local comedian with a garden demonstration. I told her this and asked how she liked Atlanta. In writing back, she was quite friendly and told me to be sure and call if I ever got through Atlanta again.

Keep your name before the editor at all times.   It is a fact that editors give assignments to writers whose names are on their minds and whose work they know. The only way you can keep your name on an editor's mind, however, is to keep that name before him or her as often as possible. This, I find, is extremely important and is something that nearly always results in assignments.

One writer I know makes it a rule to stay in constant communication. First, he offers at least one article idea a month. He also keeps track of what the editor expresses interest in—both in conversation and in the magazine itself—and then clips information on these subjects from newspapers and magazines. Then once every month or two he sends this material to that editor. In several cases after receiving the clippings, the editor has called the writer to give him an assignment on the subject, or to ask the writer to cover a different angle the writer has turned up.

Again after he's worked with the editor six months or so, he sends that editor a picture with a note saying, "We've worked together a long time, and I thought you might like to know what I look like." This writer also sends a gadget of some sort to his editors once a year. In one case, he mailed an old-style IBM card with the words, "Tension Reliever—Please Fold, Spindle, or Mutilate." At Christmas he also sends Christmas cards, which he mails at Thanksgiving so they don't get lost in the crowd.

Try to help the editor.　I personally like to help editors with their job whenever possible. In one case I knew my editor was working on a piece about buying American. On my desk I happened to have a list of authorities on this subject along with their phone numbers. I sent it with a brief note. A few days later the editor called to thank me and to say my list helped tremendously.

In another case, I knew my editor was putting together information on catalog sales, so every time I ran into an article on the subject from any source, I sent it to her. I don't know whether or not it helped, but for several years she has given me at least one assignment a month.

Now and then pick up the phone.　This is another way to keep your name before an editor. I know one writer who budgets $100 a month to call a number of magazines—because he feels it's important to keep in contact. He doesn't call, however, just to be calling. He always calls with an idea he feels is important, or he calls to let the editor know about a new development.

This doesn't always pay off in an immediate assignment, but it does help him keep in close personal contact. And currently he averages about twelve sales a year to this particular magazine.

Occasionally make a personal visit.　This same writer tries to make a personal visit to his editors once in a while. Two years ago, he made a trip around the U.S. on vacation and stopped whenever he could to talk to his editors personally.

I don't think I've ever visited an editor without coming away with an assignment or two. But there are some cautions. You shouldn't just go in. Take with you at least three or four ideas you feel might be important to that particular editor. In many cases, I've been assigned to do all the ideas I've presented as well as one or two the editor thought up while we were talking.

I have to admit that I seldom set up an appointment ahead of time. My thinking is that visiting an editor is generally secondary to the trip I'm taking. Sometimes when I'm on assignment and am in a city where one of my magazines is located, I'll call when I'm there and see if we can get together. If the editor is in and wants to see me, I have an added plus; if not, that's also okay.

However, I know that some writers call weeks ahead of time and then confirm the appointment the day before their visit. They want to make sure the editor is going to be in the office that day and isn't tied up with meetings. That's fine if your primary purpose is to visit that editor. For me, I'm always in town for another reason and never know exactly what time I'll have available until almost the last minute.

OBSERVE PROFESSIONAL BASICS

Establishing yourself with editors also has its practical side. Editors want to be able to rely on their writers and know that they'll have good material on the desk when it's due. I must admit, sometimes I have trouble doing this.

I happen to be one of those people who work well under pressure, but not so well otherwise. If I have a month to prepare the article, I'll start it ahead of time, but generally I don't get down to serious business until I can see the handwriting on the wall. Often this means the last week. As a result, sometimes I wind up sending the material by Federal Express or another carrier the day before it's due. But I always manage somehow to get the articles in on time, even if I have to stay up all night for several nights.

There are a few other things that help establish your relationship with an editor. These are covered in detail by William Brohaugh in *Professional Etiquette for Writers* (Writer's Digest Books). I will just mention a few basics.

Revise cheerfully. I have had students who become insulted when editors ask for revisions. I'm afraid that I'm on the editors' side here. I want editors to be completely satisfied with my manuscripts. If they want to change something, that's fine. If they want additional pictures, want me to call to check something, or almost anything else, I do it immediately. I suggest that you take this attitude, too. This establishes you as both a professional and as someone the editor can work with without hassle.

Give the editor enough time to reply.   Whenever you mail in a query or a manuscript, give the editor a reasonable time to respond. I know writers who are on the phone within the first two weeks to find out what happened to their query. Editors are busy people. And they will get to your material as quickly as possible.

Some magazines list their average response time in their listing in *Writer's Market*. You should expect to hear within two to three weeks of this stated response time. If a magazine doesn't list a response time, expect it to take within six to eight weeks after you mail the manuscript. After that, it is all right to write a short note that says something like this: "I mailed the query 'How to Grow Mushrooms' on January 1. Please keep it as long as you like, but I was wondering if it is still under consideration." This is non-threatening and gives the editor lots of latitude, yet it usually brings a reply.

Don't ask an editor to reconsider a rejection.   If an article comes back rejected, accept that. I have had students write nasty letters to the editor at this point, saying, "You didn't understand what I was trying to do" or "You don't know a good article when you see it." This is unprofessional. When an editor receives a letter like this, he will frequently reject further material from that writer.

SASE.   Writers and editors often insist that a self-addressed, stamped envelope is enclosed with every submission. I disagree with the practice of sending a self-addressed, stamped envelope. This is an area, however, that creates a great deal of controversy among writers and editors. These are the generally accepted rules:

Enclose a self-addressed stamped envelope any time you send in an unsolicited query or manuscript. This also applies if the editor gives you a go-ahead on a query but stipulates that it be submitted on speculation.

You do not have to enclose a self-addressed, stamped envelope when you are submitting a manuscript written on assignment or after you have sold one editor several manuscripts and have a working relationship. In addition, don't enclose an SASE when revising a manuscript at the request of an editor.

In my own case, I now work with a word processor. I often will send out as many as sixty or seventy queries a month. Since I have them on a disk and can reproduce them easily, I always indicate that I expect a reply only when they want the completed manuscript. If an editor is not interested, then I ask them to simply "throw the material away." This saves both of us a lot of trouble.

All of the tips in this chapter are designed to help you establish yourself with one editor or a number of editors so that they will accept your work on a regular basis and look to you frequently to handle writing assignments. At one time or another, I have tried all these methods. I suggest you start with those ideas that appeal to you and add to them as you begin to establish a solid writing career.

5. How to Turn Out Writing in Volume

Making a good living writing today means turning out writing in volume. The reason: the price paid per article isn't high enough to allow you to make a living by writing one or two articles a month.

Today, as we've already seen, the smaller magazines pay as little as $50 per article, medium-range magazines pay in the $200 to $800 range, and majors generally pay from $750 to $10,000 per article. Overall, the bulk of all commercial markets pay between $200 to $600 per article.

This means that if you are a full-time freelancer, you must write five to ten articles a month in the general markets to make an income of $15,000 to $25,000 a year. To do this you need to turn out articles in reasonable volume on a consistent basis. Can you do it? Of course you can. I have a lot of students who make between $6,000 and $10,000 a year writing articles part-time and a few who make $25,000 a year and more. It's just a matter of concentrating on both the quality of your work and your production.

Do you frequently find yourself plodding through your day not accomplishing what you would really like to? If so, maybe you're not using your mental capability cycle to help you get more work done.

TAKE ADVANTAGE OF YOUR PEAK WORK PERIODS

The truth is that most of us have more energy and more mental capability at certain times of the day than at others. Writing a first draft requires one type of mental capability, rewriting another, doing research another, and writing letters, filing, or reading, still another. To increase your productivity, you must match your capability level to each writing task.

Here is a system developed to increase office efficiency that has helped a number of writers turn out more work. Here are the steps:

BECOME FAMILIAR WITH THE FIVE BASIC CAPABILITY LEVELS

Level one. You're at your very best in mental energy and in your ability to create on paper. You're able to concentrate well and to work on obscure concepts. This is a good level for dreaming up article ideas, outlining, and writing first drafts. At this level, the writing process often proceeds rapidly.

Level two. Better than average level, but not quite the best. This is a good level for writing and rewriting.

Level three. The average level of good working energy. You can carry out complex activities provided you aren't trying to be your most creative. You can edit your material, write letters, put manuscripts in the mail, keep records, and do most things.

Level four. A very relaxed pleasant level if you stick to the easy and familiar. This is not the time to write first drafts or to rewrite complex material. But you can compose letters, file, read magazines, clip, follow your hobbies, and more.

Level five. This is your lowest mental energy above sleep. You don't want to write at this level, but you can file and clip. You can also relax and catch up on your reading, watch TV, and do similar things.

PINPOINT YOUR WRITING TASKS Start by listing fifteen to twenty activities you perform in connection with your writing. Here are a few:

Creating ideas (1)
Filing (4-5)
Writing first drafts (1-2)
Completing library
research (3)
Rewriting (2-3)
Analyzing articles (3)
Studying the markets (3-4)
Reading for pleasure (4-5)
Working in the darkroom
(3-4)

Interviewing by Phone (3)
Answering letters (3-4)
Interviewing in person (3)
Writing query letters (2-3)
Cleaning up office (4-5)
Reading informational
material (3)
Keeping records (4)
Clipping (4-5)

ASSIGN EACH TASK A CAPABILITY NUMBER To do this, refer to the capability levels in step one. Beside each of the activities on your list, write the number that corresponds to the level of mental energy or capability you feel is necessary to accomplish that job comfortably or well (see list).

Naturally most activities are accomplished more efficiently and quickly at higher mental energy levels. One writer finds she can write two pages of manuscript in about fifteen minutes between 9:00 A.M. and 10:00 A.M., but it takes her four times as long to turn out the same amount in the late afternoon.

CHART YOUR WRITING ACTIVITIES FOR A FULL DAY
Every hour during a particular day, take a moment to think about your level at that time. Try to separate in your mind what you feel capable of doing and what you are actually doing.

At 10:00 A.M. you might say, "I've been filing material, but I've been working out an article in my head. That means my level must be fairly high. Let's say I'm at level two mentally, but filing is a level four task."

Some writers work better at night, others in the morning. Everybody, however, starts low and rises to a peak, sometimes two or three peaks during the day, then declines. Morning people peak quickly; others take hours before they reach their highest level of the day.

When I began to rate my level hour-by-hour, I found it looked something like this.

TIME	MENTAL LEVEL	TIME	MENTAL LEVEL
7:00 A.M.– 8:00 A.M.	5	4:00 P.M. – 5:00 P.M.	4-5
8:00 A.M.– 9:00 A.M.	3-2	5:00 P.M. – 6:00 P.M.	4-5
9:00 A.M.–10:00 A.M.	1	6:00 P.M. – 7:00 P.M.	3
10:00 A.M.–11:00 A.M.	1	7:00 P.M. – 8:00 P.M.	2-3
11:00 A.M.–12:00 P.M.	3-2	8:00 P.M. – 9:00 P.M.	3
12:00 P.M. – 1:00 P.M.	3	9:00 P.M. –10:00 P.M.	3-4
1:00 P.M. – 2:00 P.M.	2	10:00 P.M. –11:00 P.M.	4-5
2:00 P.M. – 3:00 P.M.	3	after 11:00 P.M.	5
3:00 P.M. – 4:00 P.M.	3		

Now let's look at what I was doing during the day:

TIME	ACTIVITY	MENTAL LEVEL
7:00 A.M. – 8:00 A.M.	Getting up, eating breakfast, watching television, exercising.	5
8:00 A.M. – 9:00 A.M.	Straightening desk, making out daily schedule, reviewing material	3-2
9:00 A.M. –10:00 A.M.	Doing phone interviews, working on first drafts.	1
10:00 A.M. –11:00 A.M.	Writing articles	1
11:00 A.M. –12:00 P.M.	Answering mail	3-2
12:00 P.M. – 1:00 P.M.	Eating lunch	3

1:00 P.M. – 2:00 P.M.	Writing articles	2
2:00 P.M. – 3:00 PM	Writing articles	3
3:00 P.M. – 4:00 P.M.	Writing newsletter, researching articles	3
4:00 P.M. – 5:00 P.M.	Writing articles or researching	5-4
5:00 P.M. – 7:00 P.M.	Dinner	
7:00 P.M. – 8:00 P.M.	Reading, writing letters, filing	2-3
9:00 P.M. –10:00 P.M.	Working on miscellaneous projects	3
10:00 P.M. –11:00 P.M.	Working on novel	4-5

As you can see, my day basically started at 8:00 A.M. Then I began slowly by cleaning up my desk, reviewing material, and so forth. My mental energy level at this time was fairly high, three to two, yet none of the tasks required much above a four. Obviously I wasted a good hour.

For the next two hours I generally wrote. This was fine because the mental energy level required for this task and my own level coincided. Occasionally I used this time to interview by phone. However, I would have been better off spending the time writing and doing phone interviews in the afternoon.

I wasted the hour from 11:00 A.M. to 12:00 P.M. This time could have been used more efficiently if I had written articles instead of answering mail. The mail could be moved to late afternoon or evening. The rest of the day I seemed to have similar problems.

The point is to try to engage in less demanding activities at the lowest capability levels and save the higher levels for tasks requiring more mental energy. You're wasting time if you read and clip or even rewrite at level one.

After keeping track like this for several weeks, I shifted my schedule until I handled all writing at level 1-2 and rewrote at level 2-3. I also placed the rest of the tasks where they belonged. The result: my production almost doubled. Now, try the system yourself.

TIME SCHEDULE YOUR PROJECTS

In the beginning, you'll probably resist working on a schedule. But as you start turning out writing in volume, you'll suddenly realize that time is vital. Many writers, in effect, fritter their time away. Some writers who turn out one article a week could produce two a week if they used their time wisely.

To work efficiently as a writer, you must schedule. Writer Larston Farrar used to make out a list each Sunday night of the things he had to do the following week. Then each evening he made a daily list for the next day. This kept him moving ahead each day.

I personally use a different approach. I try to project out on a completion basis. Since I have a number of article and book projects running at all times, my list looks something like this:

1. Work on Rodale gardening book.
2. Work on Writer's Digest book.
3. Need query, proposal and outline for *Good Bugs* book (this is a book for gardeners on beneficial insects in the garden).
4. Work on article about classified advertising for *Fishing Tackle Trade News* magazine.
5. Work on article about retail sales techniques for *Jobber Topics* magazine.
6. Work on flower article for *Family Circle*.
7. Write universities for research sources.
8. Write students in class.
9. Finish "Invisible Market" article for *Photo Business*.

Many article and book projects will have definite completion dates established by contract or by the editor. If I don't have a firm date, I establish one. To do this, I try to estimate how much time it will take to complete a project and add fifty percent more.

I schedule that amount on my three-month calendar (see fig. 5-1). This is designed to show months, weeks, and days, as well as each work hour in the day.

Let's say it is March 5 and I have an article due on March 25. I estimate this article is going to take 8 hours to complete. I then pencil in fifty percent more time, or 12 hours. I don't necessarily fill in one solid block of time, but I often break it up. If I work on this article from 1:00 PM. to 3:00 PM. Monday, Wednesday, and Friday the first week, I'll finish it Monday of the second week. I do the same long-range scheduling for all my other projects.

This keeps all projects proceeding toward completion and should insure that I finish each before the completion date.

For projects that require letters, I drop a note in my mail basket and write them during my mail time each day.

I also make sure I keep a number of time slots open. The reason is that I frequently receive rush articles from some of my editors. In order to keep these editors happy, I must leave room for these emergency projects.

MAKE ROOM FOR DETAILS   The trouble with schedules is that sometimes you forget the little details.

I discovered I was answering the majority of mail, but not all of it, because other things came first. Sometimes an editor would call to complain I hadn't answered his letter asking that I check some detail. I also couldn't seem to find time to write for publisher catalogs for my writing class or to handle other small projects not on the schedule.

The problem was that my schedule was so tight I hadn't allowed time for any of these activities.

I could, of course, change the schedule to accommodate each individual item, but I didn't want to clutter it with such minute details as "write for publisher catalogs" or "call president of Bullock's."

The bin method.   What I did was set up three bins beside my desk. One was labeled "Mail," one—"Projects to Do," and the third—"Things to File." Then I scheduled one hour a day for answering mail and another hour every day or so for handling miscellaneous projects that are too small to schedule in, and for filing.

The mail bin now contains such notations as "write for consumer brochure," "letter to all students," "send for college resource list," "letter to publisher for possible publication of out-of-print book," and "answer requests for information."

In the project bin I have a list of magazine articles to enter in my computer information database, a note to finish the Sierra Writing Camp newsletter, a note to check with colleges about possible

3 MONTH SCHEDULE CALENDAR
(space limitations allow only a portion to be reproduced here)

	Mar 2-6					...	Mar 9-13	
	Mon	Tu	Wd	Th	Fri	...	Mon	Tu
8am- 9am	gdn-bk	gdn-bk	gdn-bk	gdn-bk	gdn-bk	...	gdn-bk	gdn-bk
9am-10am		gdn-bk	gdn-bk	gdn-bk		...		gdn-bk
10am-11am	WD-bk	FTN	WD-bk	WD-bk	WD-bk	...	WD-bk	WD-bk
11am-12pm	WD-bk	GB-qy	WD-bk	FTN	WD-bk	...	FTN	(FTN)
12pm-1pm	GB-qy	FC	GB-qy	FC		...	FC	FC
1pm-2pm	JT	Mail	JT	Mail	JT	...	JT	Mail
2pm-3pm	JT	Mail	JT	Mail	JT	...	Mail	
3pm-4pm		PB	PB		PB	...	PB	(PB)
4pm-5pm						...		

gdn-bk	Rodale gardening book
WD-bk	Writer's Digest Book
GB-qy	Query & outline for Good Bugs Book
FTN	classified advertising article for Fishing Tackle Trade News
FC	Family Circle flower article
Mail	write students/write universities—other correspondence
JT	retail sales techniques article for Jobber Topics magazine
PB	invisible market article for Photo Business
O	Completion Date

Figure 5-1. Three-month schedule calendar. A calendar like this is used to schedule all projects to completion. In practice each of these calendars is a minimum of three months long so projects can be penciled in for an entire three months. Due to space limitations this one runs for only a week and two days.

workshops, and similar items. During my scheduled hour each day I simply work on whatever is in the bin. That way I get it done easily.

In the "to file" bin I place clippings and other things that need to be stored. I work this bin when my printer is printing and when I run out of material in the project bin.

KEEP YOUR LONG-RANGE SCHEDULE FLEXIBLE

With any schedule, you need to allow for long-range changes as your writing focus shifts. I decided years ago, after working for the larger magazines, that I really did my best writing for the smaller markets in the outdoor and business trade fields. The outdoor pieces could always be written with a minimum of effort and the business trade articles usually needed only one interview.

Therefore, I arranged my schedule to accommodate this. At that time, I'd start to work about nine, work till noon, knock off till one-thirty, then work again till about six. I wrote Monday, Tuesday, and Wednesday mornings. The afternoons I reserved for photography. Thursday I set aside for interviewing. Friday I picked up the loose ends and sent off most materials.

Shifting interests.   Then in the middle seventies, my interests began to shift. I decided that I didn't like photography and that I really no longer enjoyed working on one article after another. I then began to move toward books.

Major changes always take time. I decided that since I needed to maintain my income, I would work on books in the morning and write articles in the afternoon. I also decided to do most of my research by mail and all of my interviews by phone. In the evenings I did whatever reading was needed. Over the years I made several shifts like this.

Today my work patterns have shifted again and will probably change in the future as my needs and interests widen. Therefore I try to remain flexible enough to make small adjustments as I go along, and big ones when I need them.

HANDLE ESSENTIALS ONLY   Many writers find they are

deluged with extra tasks each day. I might receive a letter from someone who has read one of my books, a request from a fellow writer for some information, or a personal letter from someone I met somewhere. It's nice to answer all mail, return all calls, send thank-you notes to people you interview, and other things. Unfortunately, I am only one person and so are you. Our main job as writers is to turn out salable material. This limits the time we spend on any other tasks.

To try to solve this "time crunch" problem, I use what might be called a rough priority system. I assign each task an A, B, and C when it comes to putting items on my schedule or in my baskets.

A's are the actual writing, revision, research gathering, interviews, and similar things.

B's are letters back to an editor, filing material, searching for ideas, and surveying magazines. These are essential but aren't directly related to getting an article out.

C's are answering a letter from a fan, revamping my file system, making personal phone calls, and similar items. As a general rule, don't perform any of these during office time. Handle A's and B's only during these periods. This helps keep your work time to production tasks only.

CHART TO FIND YOUR WEAKNESSES   The schedule itself helps focus on what you're supposed to do. But in practice, sometimes all of us slip a little and some of us slip a lot. A little slippage is no problem. But a lot of slippage is. To correct this, you need to chart yourself on an actual project basis for a day or two. Simply keep track of your movements until you decide to stop.

Be honest and write down everything you do: cleaning the room, straightening up the desk, leaning back and looking out the window, and many other things.

Here is what my work time looked like for one 4½ hour period.

8:30 A.M. – 9:45 A.M.	Cleaning up desk, straightening up books
9:45 A.M. – 10:00 A.M.	Writing
10:00 A.M. – 10:15 A.M.	Break
10:15 A.M. – 10:20 A.M.	Going in house for cup of tea
10:20 A.M. – 10:40 A.M.	Thumbing through book
10:40 A.M. – 11:15 A.M.	Writing
11:15 A.M. – 11:30 A.M.	Petting dog
11:30 A.M. – 12:00 P.M.	Writing
12:00 P.M. – 1:00 P.M.	Eating lunch

As you can see, I had gotten sloppy. When you finish making up your own chart, add the time you actually worked and the time you didn't work together. Now, divide the time you didn't work into the total time spent. That is, if you've spent two hours doing nothing during what's supposedly working time for that day and only six hours actually working, you have spent a total of eight hours. Now divide the two hours into the total (eight). This gives you a four. Now, suppose you spent six hours doing nothing and two hours working (a total of eight hours): six divided into eight equals one and three-tenths. I consider anything above a positive four satisfactory. If your score is below that, you need to improve.

The golden rule.   No matter how hard you try, you are never going to get one hundred percent work out of a day or week. Since I work at home, my wife wants me to check the car. I receive a phone call from someone to ask about writing. The school calls to ask me to pick up my son. I run out of ribbon and have to go pick up a new one.

The rule I use is: Cut down non-work activities I can control and don't worry about what I can't. That's a good philosophy if your work rating stays above positive four. If you can get six hours of good work out of an eight-hour day, that's pretty good. If you can't, then you're going to have to refuse to take phone calls: tell your wife, husband, or friends to wait until after working hours; or take whatever steps will let you spend most of your time turning out writing production.

If you're trying to write and work full-time too, the total writing time per day will be more limited. But if you can keep your productivity score above four, you'll still accomplish more than another writer with more time but less determination.

RESEARCH FROM YOUR DESK

Both researching and interviewing take a tremendous amount of a writer's time because many writers insist on traveling to find the facts they need. They also conduct a lot of their interviews face-to-face.

As far as I'm concerned, that's not okay even if the magazine is paying expenses. Why not? Because you're simply not turning out enough work for the time spent. What you must learn to do is research and interview directly from your desk. Let me first offer a few resource books that will help tremendously: *Knowing Where to Look: The Ultimate Guide to Research* by Lois Horowitz, *A Writer's Guide to Research,* by Lois Horowitz, *The Computer Data and Database Sourcebook,* by Matthew Lesko, and *How to Look It Up Online—Get the Information Edge with Your Personal Computer,* by Alfred Glossbrenner. (Full citations are listed in the Bibliography.)

SPEED UP LIBRARY RESEARCH   If you need the answer to a few questions, such as the population of Kalamazoo, Michigan, don't go to the library to look it up, call. Research librarians across the country are willing to look up basic information for you over the phone. I used to assume that every writer knew this, but when I asked my classes how many did it, only a few hands went up.

Recently, over the phone, I received the address of the firm publishing the *National Radio Publicity Directory,* discovered the number of people over sixty-five in the United States, and learned the name of the state flower of Minnesota. All of this was material I needed for my articles.

Mail order/phone research.   I have three major sources that provide me with every piece of information I could ever want. These are the government, colleges and universities, and associations and companies.

Government. The government has more information than almost anyone else, ranging from alpenhorns to zebras. There are lots of ways to tap this source. But I have a system that seems to work well.

  1. *US Government Organization Manual.* Start by going through this valuable manual, available from the Superintendent of Documents, Government Printing Office, Washington DC 20402. You will also find it in almost every library in the country.

  When I want to find information on a topic, let's say, "recreation for the aged," I go through the manual looking for every possible department that might have something to do with this subject. Generally I find a minimum of six, and sometimes as many as twenty, offices that might be able to tell me something. When I have my list complete, I write to the public information officer at each department or office and ask for any pamphlets, reports, or statistical data they might have on my subject. In several cases I have received boxes of material from one or more of the offices.

If you need quotes from an expert, call the public information officer and ask for names of authorities on a particular subject. In most cases, these people will find you an expert within a few days.

2. *Government libraries.* Washington, DC boasts numerous specialized libraries or other sources for information that can help with your research. The National Agricultural Library provides published material and research on general agriculture. The Bureau of Economic Analysis, a division of the Commerce Department, provides national, regional, and international economic statistics. The US Department of Commerce Library offers business information. And the Performing Arts Library of the John F. Kennedy Center offers reference services in any subject dealing with the performing arts. You can tap into any of these with a single phone call.

3. *Committee hearings.* Congressional committees regularly hold hearings on everything from the plight of the aging to the emigration problem. At most of these hearings, experts testify from all over the country. This information is public record and you do not need permission to quote from this material verbatim.

I have personally used this source a number of times. For an article on land fraud against the elderly, I sent for the minutes of a committee investigating these frauds and received everything I needed to complete the article, including dozens of specific cases and several hundred quotes.

Start your search here by calling the House Bill Status Office at (202)225-1772. They can tell you if any bills have been introduced covering a given topic, the status of the bill, who sponsored the bill, and what committees or subcommittees have held hearings.

Once you know which committees are holding hearings on your subject, call or write the chairman of the committee and ask for the minutes of the hearings. Generally these will be sent free of charge. Often you can also obtain the hearing minutes by requesting them from your local congressman or senator.

4. *Government computer databases.* Many government departments provide a free printout of all research contracted by their department on a particular subject. Several years ago I contacted the US Department of Health and Human Services and asked them to give me a printout on any research being conducted on "personal space." In about a month I received a printout of over two thousand research projects being financed by this department. You also can obtain these printouts by contacting the public information officer at the individual departments.

5. *Specialized databases.* In addition to these, the government also maintains a number of other individual databases. You can obtain printouts often free of charge or for a small fee. The Cancer Information Clearinghouse offers searches and printouts free of charge. The Clearinghouse on Child Abuse & Neglect Information will do free searches on all aspects of child mistreatment, and the Sample Inventory offers printouts on taxonomic information about all organisms of algae, plankton, benthic invertebrates, and fishes. You will find a complete listing of these two hundred government databases in *The Computer Data and Database Sourcebook* by Matthew Lesko.

Colleges and Universities. Most major colleges today maintain public relations offices that are happy to help writers find the information they need or to set up interviews for writers with authorities in a number of fields. A lot of these institutions maintain resources lists (fig. 5-2) that contain the names and phone numbers of authorities and specify their fields of interest.

Some colleges and universities do an outstanding job. Carnegie Mellon University sends out a weekly sheet (see fig. 5-3) that lists four or five possible article ideas you are welcome to use.

Some typical recent ideas are: "the relationship between male and female values studied by tracing the evolution of Clint Eastwood's 'super-male' image," "Carnegie Mellon psychologist David Klar says 'toddlers are capable of solving complex puz-

THE GRADUATE SCHOOL OF BUSINESS
UNIVERSITY OF CHICAGO
BUSINESS RESOURCE LIST

Fall, 1986
Contact: Public Relations

Leda Hanin
312/962-7128 (Office)
312/386-4562 (Home)

ACCOUNTING

Federal Accounting Standards
Sidney Davidson, Arthur Young Professor
of Accounting. 312/962-7136.
Roman Weil, Professor of Accounting.
312/962-7261.
Katherine Schipper, Professor of
Accounting. 312/962-7281.

Managerial Accounting
Sidney Davidson, Arthur Young Professor
of Accounting. 312/962-7136.
Roman Weil, Professor of Accounting.
312/962-7261.
Katherine Schipper, Professor of
Accounting. 312/962-7281.

BANKING AND FINANCE

Asset Pricing Theory
George M. Constantinides, Professor of
Finance. 312/962-7258.
Charles J. Jacklin, Assistant Professor of
Finance. 312/962-7324.

Capital Markets
Eugene Fama, Theodore O. Yntema
Professor of Finance. 312/962-7282.
Kenneth R. French, Associate Professor
of Finance. 312/962-7138.
Robert Hamada, Deputy Dean and
Professor of Finance. 312/962-7122.
* Richard Leftwich, Professor of
Accounting and Finance. Director,
Center for Research in Security Prices.
312/962-7266.
Robert Stambaugh, Associate Professor
of Finance. 312/962-7038.

Commercial Banking
Walter D. Fackler, Professor of Business
Economics. 312/962-7146.
John Huizinga, Associate Professor of
Business Economics. 312/962-7272.

Corporate Finance
Robert Hamada, Deputy Dean and
Professor of Finance. 312/962-7122.
Merton Miller, Leon Carroll Marshall
Distinguished Service Professor of
Finance. 312/962-7201.

Corporate Restructuring
Katherine Schipper, Professor of
Accounting. 312/962-7281.
Abbie Smith, Associate Professor of
Accounting. 312/962-7281.

Federal Reserve
Walter D. Fackler, Professor of Business
Economics. 312/962-7146.

Financial Services
Sam Peltzman, Sears Roebuck Professor
of Economics and Financial Services.
312/962-7457.

Inflation and Security Returns
Eugene Fama, Theodore O. Yntema
Professor of Finance. 312/962-7282.
Robert Hamada, Deputy Dean and
Professor of Finance. 312/962-7122.

Interest Rates
Yale Brozen, Professor of Business.
312/962-7141.
Victor Zarnowitz, Professor of
Economics and Finance. 312/962-7146.

Leveraged Buyouts
Merton Miller, Professor of Finance.
312/962-7201.
Katherine Schipper, Professor of
Accounting. 312/962-7281.

Figure 5-2. Resource List. Most universities maintain a resource or authority list. Writers who need quotes or information for their articles are encouraged to use these sources by universities' public relations offices.

Department of Public Relations
Carnegie Mellon University
Pittsburgh, PA 15213-3890
412-268-2900

You're like most consumers if you find the instruction manuals for complicated gadgets incomprehensible. "The last thing most project managers ever think about is the manual," says Carnegie Mellon Professor Erwin Steinberg. "Our Communication Design Center trains writers to be document designers—to use words and illustrations to help people use a device they really don't understand."
Contact: Kyle Fisher (412)268-3580 or 2900

Imagine the feeling of being thrust in front of a college classroom in Shanghai after only a few years of study in the Chinese language. That's the predicament many foreign graduate students face as teaching assistants (TAs) in American universities. "At Carnegie Mellon, where all foreign TAs are tested for language proficiency, the English as a Second Language program provides training in both communication and teaching skills," says Teaching Center Director Ted Fenton. "Many of these foreign TAs are brilliant scientists. We want to make sure that knowledge comes through in the classroom."
Contact: Kyle Fisher (412)268-3580 or 2900

Largely because there are no competing private forecasts, the long-term economic forecasts published by the Congressional Budget Office and the Executive branch are "consistently optimistic" no matter what President is in office, according to Carnegie Mellon's Mark Kamlet. Kamlet, who has studied federal economic forecasts from 1962-84, says private competition has tended to keep federal short-term forecasts more reliable and accurate.
Contact: Edmund Delaney (412)268-2260

Because American manufacturers face critical challenges from overseas competitors, Carnegie Mellon's business school has radically redesigned its Manufacturing Management course and has made it a required subject. Concepts such as the Japanese "Just-in-Time" philosophy, Total Quality Control, Kanban and Cycle Time Reduction are offered through case studies in which managers involved in some of these cases share their problems with students. Professor Sunder Kekre says students also visit large manufacturing facilities in Pittsburgh to study problems first-hand.
Contact: Edmund Delaney (412)268-2260

ASCEND, a computer-based modelling language developed at Carnegie Mellon, helps engineers design a model of the chemical processes in a chemical plant in hours instead of the weeks it used to take. The language works for any kind of engineering design problem, whether it be building electrical circuits or bridges, and it enables engineers to create more ideas "on paper" before building a plant, says ASCEND's creator Peter Piela.
Contact Carol Pearson (412)268-8495 or 2900

February 1987

Figure 5-3.   The Carnegie Mellon Story Idea List. This list is put out especially for freelancers. Each list contains a number of possible article ideas which writers are encouraged to use.

zles,' " and "a microeconomic model of job turnover developed by business school research helps explain why individuals change jobs."

In my own case I found an idea that read "Retailers should stop focusing on discounting, and try to sell lifestyle image to customers." I interviewed the professor for forty-five minutes and then developed a trade journal article called "Lifestyle Merchandising for the Retailer." So far, this article has sold thirteen times for a total of $2,600.

To obtain university or college resource guides or to ask to be added to the mailing lists, look up the addresses of fifteen to twenty major colleges at the library and write their public relations offices (they're called by different names at different universities).

Associations and Companies. Associations and companies offer a sometimes overlooked mail order source. The *Encyclopedia of Associations,* available at most libraries, lists over 5,000 associations that offer a wide variety of information. The *Thomas Register* lists several thousand manufacturers.

Here are a few of the listings: the American Horticultural Society provides how-to, referral and technical information on horticulture; the Bob Evans Nutritional Pet Center has information on keeping pets healthy through diet and activity; and the Women In Communications, Inc. offers historical, how-to, and trade information on the communications industry. I have found that no matter what information you need, there's at least one trade association or company that will provide it.

SEND FOR PHOTOS   I find that you can illustrate at least sixty percent of all the articles you write with photos obtained through outside sources. Sometimes, of course, you must take your own pictures, but for most general articles, you can get all the photos you need without leaving your desk.

I have illustrated hundreds of articles and a number of books with other people's pictures. Photographs for my *Family Circle* gardening articles came from the Ball Seed Company. The photos for my books *The Wonderful World of Houseboating* and *The Vegetable Gardener's Sourcebook* were contributed by several hundred companies.

You will find that practically every department of the government maintains their own picture file, sometimes running into millions of photos.

The Department of Agriculture maintains hundreds of thousands of picture files on all phases of agriculture, forests, soil conditions and homemaking. You can send for an index that lists all the subjects covered. I have found here that you should request exactly what you need. If you need a father, mother and two children picnicking in a national forest, ask for it. One of the pictures I received from them was of a child eating a bowl of strawberries.

The Still Pictures Division of the National Archives makes millions of historical photographs available, and the National Aeronautics and Space Administration offers pictures of equipment and activities of the space program.

Some agencies offer these pictures free. Others charge a small fee. See Appendix B for a list of government departments and agencies offering photos.

If you intend to use the government picture collection extensively, you will want to purchase the 275-page book *Pictorial Resources in the Washington, DC Area* by Shirley L. Green. It is available for $5.75 from the Library of Congress, Information Office, Washington, DC 20540.

SUBSCRIBE TO A COMMERCIAL COMPUTER DATABASE   You can streamline your research procedures even more by using your computer, a modem, and some of the commercial databases.

These, as you probably already know, let you tap into the index of the *New York Times,* sample all the government research on a given subject, and more.

The big three are Dialog, Bibliographic Retrieval Services (BRS), and Orbit (SDC Information Services). There are a lot of choices. See Appendix C for complete addresses and phone numbers of numerous commercial computer databases.

Knowledge Index Database, available through DIALOG Information Services, offers (1) "Agribusiness USA," a summary of articles on the business aspects of agriculture, (2) the *Academic American Encyclopedia,* which lists more than 30,000 articles and 13,000 bibliographies, (3) an index to the *Wall Street Journal,* the

New York Times, the *Christian Science Monitor,* the *Los Angeles Times,* and the *Washington Post,* (4) a magazine index, (5) Corporate News, and (6) an index to the *Harvard Business Review.* This is only a partial list of what the Knowledge Index offers. It is available for a thirty-five dollar initiation fee and a charge for the time you use.

Control Data Corporation provides an agricultural forecast, a financial consumer price index, and a lot more. If you own a computer and modem, I strongly urge you to write for additional information, then select one for regular use. My own choice is Knowledge Index because I feel it offers the most information for the least money. But of course you should check them all and make up your own mind.

TIME-SAVING TELEPHONE INTERVIEWS

In the beginning I conducted all interviews face-to-face. Today I handle ninety percent of all interviews over the phone. Last year I interviewed stock analysts, the vice presidents and presidents of forty or fifty major companies, and much more. Face-to-face I would have invested several weeks or maybe months in total travel time. With the phone I invested a total of only forty to fifty hours.

For *Western Outfitter* I wrote about twenty articles on methods used by retailers in states 3,000 miles from where I live, and I didn't set foot in the retailers' stores. In the past, I have always relied on my eyes, in a store, to pick up merchandising details. Because of this, I found the interviews a bit difficult. But I did them, and the articles turned out fine.

There are several ways to set these up. Some writers like to write the expert first, explaining they'd like to interview that person for a particular magazine. In that letter they say they will be calling at a certain time.

I personally just call, tell them what I want, and ask when would be a good time to do the interview. Most of the time they'll do it right then.

Start anywhere. When you conduct the actual interview, I suggest that you pick out five to six basic points you want to cover. Don't, however, begin with these points. Start anywhere. If a man or woman has created a successful business, my opening line usually is, "I'd appreciate it if you'd tell me just a little bit about how you got into this business in the first place." Most of the time he or she is off and running.

Use free flow when possible. Interviewees tend to talk more freely if they tell the story in their own way. I let them ramble. Whenever they approach a point I wish to cover, I make sure we talk about that subject in detail. When we finish, I check to make sure I have all the information I need. If not, I ask another question or two. Using this method I frequently obtain a lot more material than I ever could have if I had only asked ten or even twenty specific questions.

I suggest you tape-record all phone interviews, then transcribe the tapes. This takes time, but it allows you to capture all the detail and the flavor of the conversation. Naturally you should ask your interviewee if it is okay to tape.

If you are using a computer, try to type the interview directly onto the computer. This takes a bit of getting used to, but it can be done. In practice, I generally both tape and type. Then if I run behind in my typing, I still have the conversation to fall back on. Once the interview is on a computer disk, I can easily work it into my article. I find that this technique saves literally hours of time.

SHORTCUTTING WITH A COMPUTER

I work much faster with a computer than without one. I can tell you that on those rare occasions when my computer breaks down, I am in a near panic.

A computer, as those of you who own one know, lets you revise by simply moving words and chunks of material around easily. This simple step can cut your revision time in half.

But as I have discovered, not every writer saves time with a computer. Writers are funny people. I can put three writers on computers with the identical material to write and they'll finish hours apart. Why? Because the computer requires its own set of good work habits to make it a time saver.

Here are some computer writing rules I find work well.

DON'T GET INVOLVED WITH COMPUTER TECHNOLOGY Frequently when you go into a computer store, the salesman will explain that this computer has 384K RAM, two built-in 5¼ disk drives, and five expansion card slots, or whatever.

That's backward. When you start, make a list of what you need. Most writers need to work on manuscripts, revise, write multiple letters, use a spelling checker, and sometimes compile an index. Approach your hardware needs on that basis. Fortunately, most computers on the market are capable of doing all of these things with the right software.

What software? The next consideration is what software. Most writers need some sort of a word processing program and a spelling checker. And some need a filer or database manager that allows them to store some records and to turn out multiple letters, print labels, and envelopes.

Obtain those basics and you're in business. I know writers who spend a tremendous amount of time looking for the right hardware. They also go into a dither over the software and are never satisfied with what they have. Just decide what you need, buy the hardware and software that will do these functions, and learn to use them well.

As far as I can see, most word processing programs are satisfactory. I use "WordStar" and like it. But I know writers who swear by "Perfect Writer" or whatever system they started with. In most cases it's simply a matter of learning to use the system well, rather than what program you have.

After you master the basic programs, you may want to upgrade as your needs change. An article writer may want graphics. If you write books, you may want a program that will help you to index. You may also want to add a style checker or something that will point out mistakes in grammar. These are all good additions.

PUT EVERYTHING ON THE COMPUTER I know writers who still compose their first draft on a yellow pad and don't touch the computer until they are ready to begin their second draft. This is a time waster.

Learn to do everything on the computer. Why? First, it saves steps. Second, it gets you into the computer habit so that you do the entire process on the computer screen. You may not feel this is important, but I can tell you from experience that this procedure can cut the amount of time spent in writing any article or book by at least fifty percent. Any time you add steps, you slow down the process.

FINISH COMPLETELY BEFORE YOU PRINT OUT   Don't print out until you have finished your entire article. This takes a little getting used to, but do your first draft, revise it, and correct your spelling before you print out. After that, read the manuscript for typos and do the final printing.

My reason for emphasizing this is that a lot of writers write the first draft and print out. Then they make changes on the manuscript, put it in the computer and print out again. Sometimes they do this three or four times before they complete the project. This is another time waster.

TRY THE DATABASE APPROACH   Construct spin-off articles as an initial database. Let's say you expect to sell the same piece with a few minor changes to several magazines. You can, if you wish, write the piece for *Ford Times,* then write another version for the *Christian Science Monitor* and still another for an in-flight magazine.

The easiest way to do this is to write the piece first for one of your markets, say the *Christian Science Monitor.* That becomes your database. When you're ready to write the *Ford Times* and in-flight magazine pieces, you make copies of the database to other files and make the necessary changes.

In practice, when I look at a copy of my database, I can usually find only six or seven places I need to change. If it's the same piece, I just make enough changes to make the article acceptable to whatever magazine the article is meant for. This means that in a 1,500-word article I may not have to change more than 200 to 300 words in the entire article to make it acceptable for another magazine. How to resell the same article will be covered in more detail in chapter 7. If I am target slanting the idea to different magazines, I write a completely different article each time. See chapter 2 for details.

SEVEN ADDITIONAL TIPS FOR TURNING OUT WRITING IN VOLUME

In addition to the time-saving, volume-producing areas we've already discussed, there are a number of other shortcuts you can use.

1. *Set monthly dollar or volume quotas.* I work better if I have a goal or quota that I must try to reach. I recommend that you set a monthly production goal and gradually keep increasing it. I like to establish intermediate goals of six to ten pages per day and work until I have that amount finished each day. You can also say that you need to turn out a thousand, two thousand, or three thousand dollars' worth of work a month, then make sure you work only on projects that help you meet this dollar goal.

Say you've written a number of queries and you have three assignments for $400 each and one for $100, but you can only handle three assignments in a month. I would try to do all four, but if I couldn't make it, I would push the $100 project over to the next month.

I also always finish the projects that make money and let the others slip. I may be working on a new column that I intend to offer the magazines in the next few months. But if I also have four or five $300 projects to write, I work on the money-producing projects. The column gets put off until the next month.

2. *Use form letters.* One of the best ways to turn out writing in volume is to cut down on time spent writing letters. Do this by confining your original writing to longer letters and standardize the shorter ones. If you're in the habit of dropping a note to the editor with your article, why not make up one letter that will cover the general situation and send it out each time?

Now that I have a computer, I keep a model letter in a file. When I need to write a note to an editor, I simply tap into this and insert the present editor's name and address.

I have one that says "Here is the _____ article." When I need it, I simply insert the name of the article. In some cases I also insert an extra sentence or two to make the note a bit more personal.

The same applies when writing an editor for money, an organization for research material, or an authority for an answer to a question. Make up a form and use it consistently. It is a real time saver.

3. *Work toward turning out a final draft the first time.* I know a number of non-fiction writers who spend hours polishing their

writing. I also know others who never rewrite one word. Who's right? There is no right and wrong here, only that your object should be to turn out the best work you can in the shortest possible time.

To do this, try to work toward a final draft the first time. For my first draft I try to think out each sentence and each paragraph, then I write them. I also try to keep in mind that I don't want to rewrite. Most of the time I come pretty close. Then I go back and make my corrections. With the computer it's simple to make most corrections in twenty to thirty minutes.

4. *Look ahead.* Make sure that you have all the information on hand when you're ready to write. Look forward to where you want to be in six months or a year and decide what you're going to need.

This is one of my failings. For instance, I have a class coming up in "How to Write and Sell the Non-Fiction Book" this summer at Sierra Writing Camp. For this class I need publishers' catalogs and resource information from the public relations departments of fifteen to twenty universities.

The logical thing is to write several months ahead and have this material in the files when I need it. If I don't, I will have to spend extra time trying to find this material at the last minute or I will wind up not having it available at class time.

To save time, go over your project in the beginning, decide what you'll need to complete the project, and send for that material then.

5. *Combine your library time.* Instead of going to the library to research one article, always work on several at the same time and gather what you need for all of the articles at once.

6. *Use every minute.* Since writers work for themselves, it's always a temptation to fudge a bit on the time schedule. If I budget two hours to work on a project, I might well be tempted to quit five to ten minutes ahead of time and take a quick walk or to read. In addition, I often find myself wanting to go in for lunch early and not come back for an hour, or to come back a few minutes late. And I often want to quit early at the end of the day.

I added this up one day and discovered I had frittered away a total of sixty-five minutes. This was time I could have easily used to turn out an additional two or three pages of writing.

If you are on a time schedule, try not to skip out early or to come back late. Sometimes those extra few minutes of work help considerably in meeting the production goals you have set for yourself.

7. *Interview with several articles in mind.* When interviewing an expert, of course, you can't interview for two or more articles at a time. What you *can* do, however, is to ask a few extra questions that pertain to your other projects.

Let's say you're interviewing an economist for a forecast article on the state of next year's economy. But you also have an article coming up on personal finances, and maybe another on investing.

The focus of your interview is on next year's economy, but there is nothing to prevent you from asking a couple of questions that pertain to the other two articles. This way, you save additional calls and come up with good quotes that fit your other articles well.

All the tips in this chapter will help you turn out more material with less work. I have found over the years, however, that producing more is an attitude. You must want to turn out an extra article a month or to sandwich in a book project between your regular writing production. To do this, you must approach everything you do with these questions: Is there any way I can do this better and faster? How can I shortcut the process? If you will do this every day on every project and then make the necessary changes, I can promise that you will accomplish more and also feel a great deal better about your work habits.

6. How to Hit the Major Magazines

Breaking into the major magazines seems to be easy for some writers, hard for others. I know one writer who has sold more than three hundred articles, but all to magazines that pay in the two hundred dollar to six hundred dollar range. And there's probably not one name you'd recognize on the list.

I know another, however, who decided right in the beginning to crack the top markets. She picked out ten magazines she wanted to write for, studied them incessantly, and kept coming up with ideas she thought they would like. The first few times she didn't get anywhere. But gradually she began to break through, and she eventually started selling fairly regularly to *Parade* and several others.

There is little doubt that the major magazines are more selective and harder to sell articles to. After all, they get thousands of submissions every year. Magazines like *Family Circle, Playboy,* and *Cosmopolitan* receive from 5,000 to 15,000 or more manuscripts annually.

As a result, the majors demand top-notch writing. Despite this, the real barrier to publication is largely psychological. I have had students write for all of them at one time or another, including *Redbook,* and *Reader's Digest,* so I know it is possible to sell these markets regularly if you offer them the right material at the right time.

SURVEYING THE MAJOR MARKETS

Let's take a closer look at the markets we're trying to write for. I define major markets as magazines that have a circulation of 500,000 or more, pay around $1,000 per article or more, and are considered prestigious. Here is a quick run-down.

WOMEN'S MAGAZINES

Women's magazines primarily focus on fitness and self improvement, children and parents, how-to, personal finance, relationships, exposé, sex advice, true life drama, personal experiences, humor, celebrity and other profiles, current trends, travel, and other similar types.

Magazines such as *Good Housekeeping, Family Circle, Ladies Home Journal, McCall's, Redbook,* and *Woman's Day* are slanted primarily to married women who at least give equal emphasis to their families as to their careers. Each magazine has a different way of looking at the world. *Redbook* says their reader is the "juggler." She is a fairly young (median age 36.1), sophisticated reader. Their articles are aimed at helping her juggle husband, family, home, and job. You will find this type of information mentioned in *Advertising Age* and other magazines read by advertising agency personnel.

Woman's Day, on the other hand, is slanted to a married reader with a modest income. This magazine frequently runs articles on ways to save money and how to be a more savvy consumer.

Magazines such as *Cosmopolitan, Glamour, Mademoiselle, Ms. Magazine, Playgirl,* and *Self* are directed toward the single woman. Again, each of these has an individual focus. In an editorial, Helen Gurley Brown stressed that "*Cosmo* is for single women and married women who would like to be." *Glamour* is aimed at a young, college educated woman. And *Ms. Magazine* is directed toward women interested in the women's movement.

Working women have four magazines in this category: *Working Mother* and *Working Woman, Savvy,* and *Self. Savvy* says they emphasize articles covering "fashion, health and fitness—and relate all to a woman's work life." *Self* has changed from a health and fitness magazine to include stories on beauty, careers, and personal finance.

There are four fashion-oriented magazines: *Vogue* and *Harper's Bazaar, Glamour,* and *Details. Details* is a new magazine that takes the unisex approach and mixes upscale items and inexpensive "finds." There are also some miscellaneous magazines, such as *Playgirl* and *Seventeen.* The starting range for articles runs from about $750 to $2,000 and goes up from there.

SCIENCE MAGAZINES

Three magazines here could be considered majors: *Omni, Popular Science,* and *Popular Mechanics. Omni* covers a wide range of scientific subjects with a futuristic angle. We discussed the other two in some length in chapter 1. The rates range from $500 to about $1,500.

MEN'S MAGAZINES

These magazines take a great many sex-related articles, exposés, profiles, relationships, sports, current events, and similar subjects. You'll find such pieces as exposés of nuclear energy plants and the New Mafia.

Magazines such as *Cavalier, Gallery, Playboy,* and *Penthouse* are primarily pictorial magazines with articles that run 1,500 to 5,000 words. *Oui* often publishes hard-hitting exposés. *Playboy* has recently instituted changes to help make the magazine a more upscale coffee-table product. *Penthouse* publisher Bob Guccione says that his magazine has "increased its investigative reporting and is now more politically minded."

Esquire, Gentleman's Quarterly, and *Men's Guide to Fashion* are fashion-oriented. All, however, offer a wide variety of articles ranging from buying a hunting dog to sex with an ex-lover.

GENERAL MAGAZINES

The general magazines purchase articles on a wide variety of subjects, but unfortunately, there are only a few major publications in this category: *Life, National Geographic, TV Guide, Reader's Digest,* and the *Saturday Evening Post. Signature,* the Diner's Club magazine, also pays in this range. The *Saturday Evening Post* takes how-to's, health articles, and celebrity interviews. *Na-*

tional Geographic runs articles on science, natural history, exploration, and geographical regions. Payment ranges from $1,000 to $10,000. Study individual magazines carefully before querying.

HOME AND GARDEN MAGAZINES

Better Homes and Gardens, House and Garden, House Beautiful, and *Metropolitan Home* could be considered major magazines in the home and garden field. *House and Garden* takes very little freelance material. *House Beautiful* accepts how-to remodeling, a little humor, interviews, and profiles. *Better Homes and Gardens* runs articles on education, money management, home entertainment, education, and other subjects compatible with the magazine. *Better Homes and Gardens* pays poorly considering its advertising revenue and circulation, but it is included as a major magazine because it is prestigious.

I have not listed *Country Living* in this category because its rates just don't measure up to major league standards for a magazine with a million plus circulation.

Although rates even for the majors in this category tend to be low—about $300 to $600 per article—this is a field that's quite open to first-time writers. So it's still worth considering if you have appropriate article ideas.

NATIONAL SUNDAY SUPPLEMENTS

Parade magazine isn't as good a market as it used to be. Many of their articles are written by their staff or by their contributing editors like Cleveland Amory and Michael Ryan. They publish provocative national pieces and a lot of interview and celebrity pieces in various fields. A recent celebrity article featured world champion women's figure skater Debi Thomas.

SPORTS/OUTDOORS MAGAZINES

You'll find four major magazines in the sports and outdoors fields: *Field and Stream, Outdoor Life, Sports Afield,* and *Sports Illustrated.* The outdoor magazines specialize in hunting, fishing, camping, and other outdoor interests. *Field and Stream* has expanded its coverage to include outdoor cooking and some outdoor wear. *Outdoor Life* is considered the magazine of technique—the what's new, how-to, where-to-go publication of the field. It has also expanded its coverage of outdoor wear and food. *Sports Afield* sometimes features articles on conservation, camping, and photography. A recent article examined the art of stalking—not necessarily killing—animals.

Sports Illustrated covers all sports areas. It is mostly staff-written, but it buys especially regional material from freelancers. The rates of the big three outdoor magazines are low for their advertising revenues—in the $500 to $600 and slightly up range. *Sports Illustrated* pays $1,500 and up for national articles and $500 to $1000 for regional articles.

OTHER MAGAZINES

Travel and Leisure has a circulation of almost a million and pays reasonably well, usually from $750 to $2000. They use articles on travel and destinations, restaurants, shopping, and sports. This magazine is a little hard to hit since they assign most articles, but it's worth trying if you write travel articles.

POOR PAY RATES

The major magazines admittedly pay better than all others, but the pay rates are miserly even in the best markets. Why? The cover prices of magazines and magazine advertising rates have skyrocketed in many areas over the last fifteen years, but the rates paid writers have barely inched up.

In 1987, article rates between $750 and $3,000 are common but unfair when you consider each magazine's advertising revenue. Advertising page rates for major magazines currently run between $40,000 to $150,000 and more per page. Several years ago when I was a member of the Association of Business Writers of America (ABWA), we worked on establishing an article rate of between 1/8th and 1/4 of an advertising page rate. That is, if a magazine receives $2,000 a page for its advertising, a fair rate for an article would be between $250 and $500. At that time I had no trouble convincing most editors in the trade field that this was fair.

So far as I know, however, no one has been able to establish an article/advertising page rate link for the major magazines. This would mean that the majors would have to offer a writer between $5,000 and $37,500 per article and more. The actual rate would vary with each magazine.

Is this fair? I think so. Consider today's cost of living, the salaries paid most professionals, and the time of apprenticeship most writers must put in before they can sell these magazines on a regular basis. I know a few professionals who have become polished enough to work regularly for major magazines with only three to four years' writing experience, but many others I know have spent ten years or more just breaking in.

What are the chances of rates going up? Not very good since the writer has no leverage. Rates must go up, however. Most writers I know feel that current article fees (for major magazines) are at the very least 500 to 600 percent below where they should be. A number of professionals with many years' experience are leaving the field because they can no longer make a reasonable wage writing articles.

What can you do? The only thing an individual writer can do is to keep pushing. Ask for more at every opportunity, and express your opinion that the rates are too low. While the rates for articles written for the smaller magazines are also modest, they are pretty well in line considering the income of these publications. The culprits here are the majors.

BECOMING FAMILIAR WITH INDIVIDUAL MAGAZINES

If you expect to write for the "bigger" magazines, you must analyze both the types of articles they carry and the overall magazine's style much more carefully than you would for the general market. Here is a system I have used in classes for a number of years that gives you an x-ray look at these publications.

Start with your reader. Demographics are all important to the major magazines. Most, as I've already mentioned, conduct extensive studies as to who the readers are. They also spend considerable time trying to decide what kinds of articles these readers will respond to. From these studies, they work out the approach the magazine will take.

Become familiar with these readers. Ask yourself: Are the readers men, women, or a mixed audience? What is their age range? Their income? Are they married? Single? How do they approach life? What kind of cars do they own? How big are their houses?

What are their occupations? What church would they most likely attend? What do they do for a living? Are they blue collar? Professionals? Yuppies? How are they likely to dress? What music do they listen to? What would their next purchase be? Add anything else you can think of. When you finish, sum up who this reader is in two to five sentences.

Here's an example: This reader is a modern woman who seems to be part of today's technology in a big way. She knows a great deal about microchips, buys her own car, and has a sharp eye for performance and value. She's probably about thirty-five, married, with a family income of $35,000 plus. She's a tough, demanding consumer who likes to dress well, buy the best, and pamper herself at times.

Once you have created a picture like this, you can easily visualize what articles this woman would want to read.

Make a list first of the article types the magazine offers its readers.   Are the articles how-to, informational, investigative, inspirational, interview, personal experience, nostalgia, profile, personal opinion, or roundup? Now list every title published under each article type that you find in six to twelve issues of the magazine.

Pick the categories that interest you and study those categories carefully.   You may find several article types under each category. You practiced doing this in chapter 2. You need to repeat the procedure here.

Family Circle frequently runs articles in a category that I call "How Parents Cope with Children's Problems." Here are three titles from that category:

" 'Every Mother's Fear: Abduction' (An estimated 1.8 million children will be reported missing this year. What can you do to protect your child?)"

" 'The Early Years When You Have More Than One' (Two or more children can make your life merrier, but also more complex. If you sometimes feel that you're spreading yourself too thin, relax—finding enough time and energy to go around may be more manageable than you think)."

" 'How to Talk to Your Kids About Sex' (From the innocent 'Where do babies come from?' to the more difficult 'Ma, what is a homosexual?', kids' questions pose a tremendous challenge. But you can turn those awkward situations into moments that bring you closer)."

Write two or three sentences that sum up the treatment. Here is my statement covering the above articles: "Generally one of these articles is a semi-investigative piece. The first third explains the problem using statistics and quotes from authorities to prove the point. The last two-thirds is basically how-to. That is, it tells the parent what to do to solve the problem."

"The other two articles explain the problem in about two hundred words, then use a question and answer format to explain to parents how to handle the problem."

This, of course, is a small sample, but it gives you a fairly good idea of how this magazine handles this kind of article.

Practice coming up with article ideas you feel might fit these categories. At this point, I find it extremely helpful to practice creating ideas that might fit some of the categories or areas the magazine covers. Sometimes I'll create as many as twenty or thirty. I don't try to judge what I have done. I simply spin them out. Here is some of my thinking on the problems parents have with children:

The first idea that pops into my mind is the experience of a small child going to school for the first time. There's an adjustment here that's sometimes traumatic. In my own case, when my child started kindergarten, it was such a shock that he refused to talk to the teacher or the other children for six months. Let's try this out with the title "How to Help Your Child Adjust to School."

Here are some other possibilities I dreamed up: "Ten Ways to Help an Underachiever," "How to Handle a Rebel," and "What If You Suspect Your Child is Being Molested." Now see if you can create your own.

Analyze article construction carefully. Use the form from chapter 4, page 60. When you finish this exercise you will have a basic idea of the reader, the magazine's idea focus, the types of articles they take, and the construction of individual articles.

THE EASIEST ARTICLE

Don McKinney, former managing editor of *McCall's* states in an article in *Writer's Digest* that the true-life drama is in great demand and is one of the easiest ways to break into a major magazine.

In the article he explains how a friend of mine, Paul Bagne, made his first sale to *McCall's* with an article about a young woman who had been told at age fourteen that she had leukemia.

The girl tried a radical new medical treatment on the recommendation of her doctor. This treatment eventually sent the disease into remission. Later she fell in love and married but was told that if she were able to get pregnant, it might cause the disease to return. She did become pregnant, and both she and the baby came through with flying colors.

Stories that describe a dramatic experience in the lives of real people are extremely popular today. Readers identify with these people and also receive inspiration and courage from them. As a result, editors constantly search for them. You will find these in *Life, Reader's Digest, Ladies Home Journal, Family Circle, Woman's Day,* and many other magazines.

Other true-life dramas that appeared in *McCall's* include a piece about a girl with birth defects who had been falsely labeled retarded and was placed in a state institution where a nurse rescued her, and a story about a woman who developed multiple sclerosis and lost the use of her legs and arms, yet fought back and went on to run a 26.2-mile marathon.

In looking through *Woman's Day,* I see articles on a grandmother's search for her grandson and a woman's true story about raising a disabled child. *Family Circle* recently ran true-life dramas about a mother who learned from the experience of caring for a son with an incurable disease, a woman and her husband who survived a hijacking, and a woman's brave recovery from a stroke. You need to stay current with what the magazines take by continually reading the true-life drama articles in the publications you wish to write for.

EXPERIENCES TO LOOK FOR   Here are three types of stories that magazines commonly run.

1. *An extraordinary experience.* This involves some sort of disaster that places a person in jeopardy. The article tells how he or she comes through safely.'

Example: A skin diver searching for gold in California's Mother Lode has a boulder roll over on him and pin him underwater within a few inches of the surface. The story tells how a passerby kept diving underwater to save his life by giving him air, mouth-to-mouth, until he was rescued several hours later.

2. *A common problem.* This story describes how a person dealt with a significant problem. This helps others in similar circumstances understand how they might handle the same types of difficulties.

Example: A man tries to obtain custody of his eight-year-old daughter when the parents' marriage ends in divorce. The mother accuses him of molesting the daughter. He is routed out in the middle of the night and thrown in jail. After a trial lasting several months, he proves his wife has falsely accused him.

3. *A national issue.* This usually deals with something in the news that is a recurring issue. This could involve topics like abortion, environmental pollution, the homeless in America, and unemployment.

Example: A prospective father petitions the hospital to keep his brain dead girlfriend on a life support system until their baby is born. The girlfriend's parents and the hospital refuse. He obtains a court order to keep the mother "clinically alive" until the birth of the baby. A healthy child is delivered a few weeks later.

To write this type of article, let the formats of the true-life dramas in each individual magazine be your guide. Often the story will tell itself. The lead is usually anecdotal and starts in the middle of the problem or at some very dramatic moment. Make sure to include lots of detail. See page 61 for an example of an anecdotal lead.

Where do you find these stories? Everywhere. Many of them are covered in the local papers. In my area the newspapers ran a story of a local TV newscaster who was hit by a stray bullet and paralyzed. She is in a wheelchair, but is fighting back with gusto and is well on her way to becoming a productive member of society.

Sometimes you'll hear about them in casual conversation, on local TV shows, and from doctors. Frequently, also, you can turn up true-life dramas by digging deeper into newspaper articles on other subjects. Maybe you read about a medical breakthrough, you hear about the tragic results of a particular disease, or a certain type of injury case keeps turning up in the media over and over. It's then your job to dig through these cases and sort out the individual true-life drama that a magazine might be interested in.

I personally have never written or sold one of these articles. But ninety percent of all of my students who break into the major markets do it with the true-life drama.

This is also the experience of a friend of mine, Bud Gardner, who teaches article writing at American River College in Sacramento. His students have sold thousands of articles, including a number to *Reader's Digest.* Practically every sale to the majors has been a true-life drama. If I were trying to crack the more prestigious markets today, that's probably where I would start.

SPECIAL DEPARTMENTS AND BACK-OF-THE-BOOK PIECES

Sometimes special departments and the short back-of-the-book pieces provide an easier entree to the major magazines than do the longer, more fully researched pieces.

Savvy solicits articles in the following departments: "Tools of the Trade" (ideas and strategies for doing business better), "Brief Encounters" (essays on the personal lives of worldly women), "Career Strategies," "Executive Etiquette," and "Health." *Savvy* also runs first person problem solvers.

Glamour looks for opinion essays for its "Viewpoint" section. The "His/Hers" column features essays on relationships and comments on current mores.

Woman's Day runs several short 400- to 600-word pieces on housekeeping and solving individual problems in the back of the book. These are not listed in the Table of Contents. A few of the recent ones: "Speedy Barbecue Cleanups," "Hard of Hearing? Try These Do-It-Yourself Gadgets," "More for Your Microwave," "Cost Efficient Ways to Let the Light Shine," and "Write You Are" (handwriting analysis).

Woman's Day also runs a back page called "Reflections." These are essays on matters of concern to women. Here are some recent ones: " 'Do Your Kids a Favor—Hold the Lavish Bouquets!' (Yes, too much criticism can crush a child's spirit. But I question the wisdom of indiscriminate applause)," " 'Just Call Us Nouveau Traditional' (Our Thanksgiving gathering is small—even counting the holiday bird. But we're not short on customs; we're making up our own as we go)." " 'In Praise of Snow White' (To someone without kids, motherhood may look like chaos. But inside almost every mom lurks a highly competent efficiency expert)," and " 'Double Trouble' (Some people in this world believe that wasting time is no sin. Then there are the rest of us)."

You will find these departments and back-of-the-book pieces in many of the major magazines. Many editors point out that it's often easier to make a sale here the first time out. *Travel and Leisure* recommends that new writers try ideas that fit one of their six regional editions. And *Sports Illustrated* advises that newcomers try for the regional text under the following headings: "Shopwalk," "Footloose," "Viewpoint," "Sideline," "On Deck," "Spotlight," "Sports Rx," "Replay," "Update," "Stats," "Yesterday," "Nostalgia," "Reminiscence," "Perspective," "First Person," and "On the Scene."

To write for these departments or to contribute short back-of-the-book pieces, you again need to analyze these sections carefully. You will find most of these listed under the individual magazines in *Writer's Market*.

WATCH FOR EDITORIAL CHANGES

Today our society seems to be in a state of constant change. Currently there are over forty-three million women in the workforce. Married women who work account for fifty-nine percent of all female workers. More than three million women hold executive or managerial positions, 702 thousand now run their own business, and a growing number of working couples have combined incomes of $50,000 or more. In addition, men are assuming a greater part of the responsibility for raising the children, and joint custody of children in divorces is starting to become common.

These changes and others have caused magazines to shift formats as they struggle to keep up with the needs of their readers. Recently *Woman's Day* began to bill itself as "America's personal news magazine for the woman with the twenty-six-hour lifestyle." In studying it, I have been able to find a shift to stronger points of view and more impassioned opinions in the articles. It also now seems to be carrying one career-oriented story in every issue.

Several years ago *Woman's Day* featured self-help medical articles. Now the medical pieces appear to be more informational and, in many cases, are bylined by an MD. Other magazines have undergone similar changes, either to keep up with the readers or to carve out a new demographic territory.

Change of any sort in a magazine often represents opportunity for a freelance writer. It usually means that the magazine will need additional material for the new departments or categories.

I watch carefully for these changes because I nearly always make additional sales at this time. Years ago, as I mentioned in chapter 2, when the magazine *American Home* started a California edition, I made one quick sale because they needed something immediately, then I went on to become a regular correspondent for several years. Since that time, I have been able to break into a number of magazines using this technique.

Recently one of the magazines I work for switched from a weekly magazine to a monthly. In the process they expanded the coverage considerably, cut down on spot news, and began to run longer features. The minute I became aware of this, I sent the editor a list of twenty possible articles I thought would fit his new format. As a result, I have been selling the magazine one article an issue for the past several months.

When you are trying to sell a particular magazine, you need to read every issue and watch for these changes. Sometimes you will find listings of new departments or directions in current market directories. They are, of necessity, however, several months behind. You can stay more current by regularly reading such magazines as *Writer's Digest* to keep an eye out for announcements of new or additional editorial needs. As I've already mentioned, *Advertising Age* and other magazines read by advertising agency personnel often telegraph changes far ahead of the writer's magazines.

If you hear about a change and want to know which editor is handling that department, by all means put in a brief call to the magazine's receptionist and ask. You will find the magazine's phone number listed on the masthead. If you intend to write a letter and aren't sure of the correct editor or how the editor's name is spelled, ask for that also.

WHAT TO INCLUDE IN MAJOR MAGAZINE QUERIES

Like all queries, a query to a major market is a selling letter and should be restricted, if possible, to one page. This query has a two-fold purpose: to convince an editor that you have a good idea for the magazine and to obtain the editor's confidence in your ability to handle the article.

A good query contains these points:

- The title of the article.
- The hook.
- A description of the subject.
- How you will handle the subject.
- Your qualifications.
- A request for the sale.

THE TITLE   The title should help create interest in the article. This means you should try to show an angle (preferably a unique angle) which convinces an editor that this article might fit the format and be of interest to readers.

Examples: "How Not to Lose Friends Over Money," "Great Ways to Earn $25,000," "Housewives in Space," "Kidney Dialysis: A Taxpayer's Nightmare," and "Living It Up in Debt."

THE HOOK   This is designed to snag the editor's interest and to make him or her read on. This is the lead paragraph and should have a solid impact. In most cases you should limit this "hook" to one paragraph. It can be written as a question, an anecdote, a striking statement, a statistical summary, or any number of other forms, but it often relates a problem to be solved or offers something unusual or striking about a subject.

Example 1:   "In Oregon, a nine-year-old girl was beaten about the head. She is still recovering, six years later. In New York, a teacher with an axe terrorized a classroom. Isolated incidents? Not according to . . ."

Example 2: "Did you know that your feet will carry you some 65,000 miles during your lifetime? That they contain one-fourth of all the bones in your body? That they balance, turn, and spring with perfect precision in every movement and position? Our feet are truly priceless parts of our bodies that cannot be replaced. Yet according to experts, foot disorders appear to be one of your most neglected health problems today."

A DESCRIPTION OF THE SUBJECT   Don't suggest a general area like personal finance, consumerism, or the liability insurance problem. As Rebecca Greer, editor of *Woman's Day,* points out, "It has to be more persuasive than that." Propose a specific idea that has a main point and an angle that will interest the magazine. What do you want your readers to get out of this? What is your point of view? Pro? Con? Objective? This should be covered in one or two paragraphs. It should offer an overall look at the subject along with the angle and also present a specific example if it is appropriate.

Example: "Nobody knows how many there are for sure: Americans with their lives destroyed by false charges of child abuse—physical, emotional, and sexual. Douglas Besharov, founding director of the National Center on Child Abuse and Neglect, says 'The system today is making 750,000 inappropriate investigations a year.' The false charges are bundled vaguely into Besharov's catchall figure. But it is significant that a 1984 grass roots movement of victims has spread like a prairie fire with 160 VOCAL chapters in forty-seven states. Besharov, who helped write the first mandatory child abuse reporting laws, now compares the system he helped create to 'a 911 emergency system which cannot distinguish between a murder and littering.' "

HOW YOU INTEND TO HANDLE THIS SUBJECT   First, you should give a quick overview of what you intend to include in your article. Then, tell the sources of your material, stating clearly whether the article will be based on your own experience, statistical reports, interviews with authorities, scientific studies, or another source.

Example 1: "In this piece, I'd like to go into some of the loco-motives and rolling stock of the Roaring Camp railroad (its history, where it operated, etc.), how it is being authenticated, how the village can be reached, and other colorful details."

Example 2: "Using information from several major studies and from interviews with nationally known authorities, I will explain the advantage of school-based health clinics, show how parents can help kids develop new attitudes and feelings, explain how community programs are helping pregnant teenagers stay in school, give examples of how the media can help, show parents how to arrange group programs that help improve communication between themselves and their children, and offer sources for more information."

YOUR QUALIFICATIONS Editors generally expect to be sold on your qualifications to write this piece. You don't have to have a degree in the subject to be an authority. If it is an article on Italian cooking, for instance, the fact that you've collected Italian recipes for years, have become known for your Italian cooking, and understand the subject backward and forward are perfectly good qualifications.

Go back through your life and answer these questions:

Does your present or former job give you any special credentials for writing the article? If you have been a teacher, you certainly have the qualifications to write a piece on parent-teacher relations or any number of related subjects. Teaching workshops, seminars, or classes in specialized subjects adds to your expertise.

Do you have any education in this field? Have you taken any classes that qualify you to write on this subject? I find that my degree in botany helps qualify me to write garden or horticulture articles. Classes in family counseling could qualify you to write pieces on family problems. An advanced degree also helps give you the status of an expert.

Do you have any specialized interests or hobbies? Maybe you garden, collect coins, have clipped news stories and articles on one particular celebrity for several years, climb mountains, ski, or specialize in cheesecake recipes. All of these help contribute to your expertise in particular fields.

Does your family or personal life give you some special insights? Maybe you've helped a child who doesn't get along well with other kids, raised a child with a handicap, had a teenager join a cult and disappear, or gone through a problem with a mate. These would help give you special insights when writing articles on those subjects.

I suggest you take a piece of paper and list anything in each of these categories that pertains to the article you are writing. Then write a paragraph on your qualifications. Include four or five reasons why you're qualified to write this article. Within the confines of one paragraph, four or five different qualifications make you sound extremely experienced.

Example: "I have worked for five years as the only female mechanic in a garage; I have also taught several courses in auto mechanics for women and have written a number of articles on this and related subjects."

Sometimes a writer will list some of the articles they have written, and even include a photocopy of a printed article. This is okay if the articles have something to do with the topic you are writing about and help enhance your qualifications. However, listing or including an article on gardening when you are querying about a true-life drama seems like a waste of time to me. It is better in these cases to generalize. Simply say, "I have written a number of articles for other publications," or something similar. In a similar vein, don't tell the editor anything about yourself that doesn't relate to the article you intend to write. He or she doesn't want to hear about your history, family ties, or degrees unless that information is absolutely necessary to establish you as an authority on a particular subject.

A REQUEST FOR THE SALE

Example: "If you're interested, I'd be glad to send the article on speculation." Here, on speculation means that you will send the article in on an approval basis. If the editor likes the article, he or she will buy it. If not, you'll get it back. With this approach, there is no assurance that the magazine will buy your article. You can also use the phrase "please let me know about this."

Also be sure to slant your query directly into the magazine's focus. Sometimes it should talk in the language of the publication. With *Popular Science,* as we've already mentioned, emphasize the latest in new developments. With *Cosmopolitan,* you should be slightly flamboyant. Read each magazine carefully to see how they relate to their audience.

Instead of writing your query in the style of the magazine, you can simply state that it will be a first person account and whether it will be scholarly, chatty, informal or another style. (See figure 6-1 for a sample query.)

WHY YOUR QUERY MIGHT BE REJECTED

Queries are rejected by major magazines for a number of reasons:

Your article idea may already be assigned to another writer. I have suggested articles many times only to be told they just assigned it or that the magazine has substantially the same article waiting for publication. Queries are also rejected because the magazine has published similar pieces in the recent past.

It may also be rejected because you have suggested ideas that are completely inappropriate. This varies all the way from suggesting articles the magazine never publishes to failing to offer the proper slant on a subject.

The query itself may be poorly written. This may mean you failed to put your message across clearly, or you didn't include the necessary information. In class, I often see queries that forget to give the proposed article a title. They fail to state what the article will be about. They don't detail how they are going to handle the piece. Or they don't convince the editor that they are qualified to write the piece.

To avoid this, after you write the query, make sure it covers the six major points. If any of the points seem weak, rewrite until you're satisfied you've done a superior job. If you are interested in writing top quality query letters, I suggest that you make *How to Write Irresistible Query Letters* by Lisa Collier Cool part of your reference library.

August 23, 1983

Lisel Eisenheimer
Assistant Managing Editor
McCall's
230 Park Avenue
New York, NY 10169

Dear Lisel Eisenheimer,

Cindy Halbert is alive, healthy and pregnant. Her baby is due next week. "When I told the obstetrician my medical history," she said on the phone, "he almost fell out of his chair."

Eight years ago, Cindy was a teenager fighting for her life. Stricken with deadly Acute Myeloid Leukemia, doctors expected her to live six months, maybe a year. If she recovered, against all odds, they warned that drugs used in therapy might make her sterile. "That part really bothered me," she recalled. "I had always pictured myself with kids." For five years physicians attacked-- with harsh chemicals--the cancer cells in Cindy's blood. She and her mother remember times when she lingered near death.

The personal narrative I propose for McCalls would contrast the trauma of her struggle to live with her joy in giving birth. As part of Cindy's story it could also report on medical advances in treating leukemia.

I know Cindy through my volunteer work with the American Cancer Society. Two medical sources have agreed to do interviews for this article: William Lande, one of Cindy's doctors, now a professor of pediatrics at UC San Francisco and Stuart Seigel, a renowned specialist in childhood leukemia at UCLA.

My credits include the Los Angeles Times Syndicate, the San Francisco Chronicle and the investigative journal Mother Jones. Please let me know if you want this story. I'll drop you a note on the baby's health as soon as it's born.

Sincerely yours,

Figure 6-1.   Major magazine query. This query resulted in a first time sale to Mc-Call's magazine.

RECHECK YOUR ARTICLE BEFORE YOU SEND IT OUT

Your article should always be the best you can possibly make it. After I have my article nearly ready to go, I always run through it once more to see if I think it measures up to magazine standards and to see if I can improve it in any way.

MAJOR FLAW CHECKLIST   Here is an article checklist that will help you pick up major flaws. Use this one along with the one in chapter 4.

1. *Beginning.* Leads ordinarily are one to three paragraphs long and consist basically of two parts—a curiosity arousing hook to catch the reader and a transition into the body of the article. See pages 60-64 for a more complete discussion of leads.

2. *Organization.* This is probably the most important part of an article and is the reason why some articles are hard to read, others clear and logical. I've never held to an organizational formula, but I believe the parts must be arranged in a logical order. The procedure simply is to decide on five or six elements that belong in the article, then shift the elements around until they logically proceed from one point to the other.

3. *Theme.* Is the theme or main idea apparent and consistent throughout the article? Does every paragraph relate in some way to the theme?

4. *Anecdotes, statistics, and quotes.* Are they smooth and well-done? Are they the same type and are they present in about the same percentages as in similar articles in the magazines?

5. *The writing.* Say it in the fewest number of words. Use common, direct words, use active verbs instead of inactive, and use picture words. Unfortunately since this is not a book on how to write I can't go into the details of rewriting here. I would like to recommend a short but mighty book, however: *How to Write* by DeWitt H. Scott. (See Appendix A for the address.)

6. *Style.* Does your article use the same language or style of similar articles in the magazine? If the magazine's articles are flamboyant, formal, talky or whatever, yours should be written the same way.

7. *Ending.* Make a survey of the endings used in similar articles in the magazine. Article endings include the lead replay, restatement of purpose, summary, quote close, anecdotal, straight statement, and others. Do you end yours in about the same way?

BREAKING THE PSYCHOLOGICAL BARRIER

Like everybody else, writers somehow seem to fall into a rut. I know writers who have written hundreds of articles to the minor and specialty magazines but never seem to be able to hit the bigger ones. Some of them tell me that they feel like there is a solid barrier between them and the bigger markets.

I do know from personal experience that the more you become entrenched in the lower pay markets the more unobtainable the majors seem to be. I'm not sure I can tell you why, but I know that this is true. In most cases, I find this can be overcome by becoming as comfortable as possible with the idea of writing for these markets.

If you also have this problem, I suggest you immerse yourself in the major magazines you would like to write for. Read these publications from cover to cover several times and do the surveys recommended in this chapter.

Finally, pick out an article or two that you think you could have written, then try to imagine what you would have gone through to write that particular article. What sources would you have tapped to do the research? Would you structure your piece the same way? Would you have used similar anecdotes or could you have improved on the ones in the article? What would you do to improve this piece?

Next, schedule some time each day to work on nothing but the major magazines. This can be as little as fifteen minutes a day. The important thing is to actually create article ideas designed for these magazines, to write the queries, and to send them out.

Some writers also find they can break the psychological barrier with simulated experience. That is, they see themselves writing the articles for particular magazines, see the published articles in the magazine, and try to feel what's its like to negotiate with these editors and to actually have their articles appear in print.

Use whichever method works best for you. The important thing is to try to become comfortable with the idea of publishing in the major magazines, so that you don't create a mental barrier for yourself.

No matter what you do, there are some magazines that you probably will never hit. I suggested articles to *Family Circle* for many years. Unfortunately I never received a go-ahead. I quit trying for several years, then wrote a couple of gardening books that were taken by the Book of the Month Club. After that I began getting requests for articles on this subject from several magazines and soon placed several of these in *Family Circle*.

There are fortunately enough magazines so that if you can't seem to interest the editor of one particular publication, you may well be able to attract the attention of another.

Selling to major magazines is really not much different than selling to the smaller publications. Major magazines may be harder to hit, the articles may be longer and often require more thorough research than the articles in some of the smaller markets, but the plus is that the editors of major magazines are always looking for good articles. And once you show them that you can turn out these pieces consistently, you can be sure that the welcome mat will always be out.

7. Selling the Same Article Many Times

Can you actually sell the same article over and over? Of course you can. It's like everything else in the writing business; however, you can do it only under certain conditions and in certain specialized markets. You cannot sell the same piece to ten or fifteen different women's magazines, to all of the big three outdoor magazines, nor to any other magazines that compete with each other for readers. The one thing an editor hates most is to pick up a copy of a competing magazine and find an article there that he just ran. When this happens, you can be sure the writer of the article will never sell to either of those magazines again.

There are some publications, however, that don't mind buying articles that have appeared elsewhere. The reason is that these magazines serve specific groups of readers. They have no objection if you sell the same article to a publication that their readers will never see. These are called "non-competing" publications because they don't compete with each other for readers.

What you are reselling here is the exact same article. This is quite different from reslanting (target slanting) the material for different markets. Target slanting is covered in chapter 3.

In most cases it is possible to photocopy these articles many times and simply send them out. The primary exception is articles sold to trade journals and non-competing general publications. In some cases, these are changed slightly to take into account particular readerships, I'll explain how later in this chapter. This is still considered reselling the same article, not reslanting or target slanting.

You can often sell the same article a number of times within six groups of publications. They include newspapers, regional magazines, non-competing general magazines, juvenile religious magazines, global magazines, and trade journals.

NEWSPAPERS

Newspapers buy literally thousands of features every year on a wide variety of subjects from British gardens to whale watching. You can tell which newspaper features have been provided by freelancers by a notation just under the author's name that says, "Special to the *Chicago Tribune*," "Special to the *LA Times*," or whichever newspaper it happens to be.

Because I have students who specialize in selling newspaper features, I frequently clip articles from several of them each week just to keep track of what's being purchased. Believe me, the variety of subjects is mind-boggling.

A COLLECTION OF SUBJECTS

I recently found the following titles in my files: "Sprucing Up Your Car with a Used-Car Dealer's Finesse," "Biking Norman Rockwell Country," "Antique Tools—Growing Interest in a Young Field," "Family Papers—Proper Conservation Saves Treasures," "Ballooning: Thrilling, Invigorating, and Elemental," and "Ancient Teeth Yield Clue to Origin of Oldest Inhabitants of America."

Can articles like these be sold to a number of different newspapers? The answer is yes. After all, newspapers have only a limited circulation area. Some newspapers cover all or most of a state; others may serve a region or a single county; still others have a readership limited to one city and its outlying population area.

Most newspapers are perfectly willing to let you resell an article outside their circulation area. This means you can sell the same feature to the *Seattle Times,* the *San Francisco Chronicle,* the *Salt Lake Tribune,* the *Kansas City Star,* and other newspapers.

Several years ago, a friend of mine wrote a 1,200-word article on the many uses of computers. The first year he sent his computer article to about two hundred major, daily, noncompeting newspapers across the US. This resulted in sales to the *Denver Post* and a number of others. Payment, however, was extremely uneven and ranged from as low as $30 to a high of $120. The total for the first year was about $900.

The second year he sent the same article out to about two hundred smaller newspapers across the country, including the Bangor *Daily News,* the Jackson *Daily News,* the Montana *Standard,* and others. This time around, he picked up about $600.

The third year he mailed to weekly newspapers. This round netted only $300. The fourth year he started all over again with the state-wide newspapers.

Another writer, George Beinhorn, has had extremely good luck with an article on poison oak and poison ivy. The first year, George figured, he took in about $900. He then decided to get extremely scientific about it. From *Bacons Publicity Checker* (see the Bibliography for the address) he put together a list of about 1,200 newspapers.

These he divided into state-wide papers, regional or metro papers, local papers, and lower levels of non-overlapping circulation. He entered this list on a computer disk. His object was to use a mailmerge program to automatically address both his cover letter and his mailing labels. This, he hoped, would allow him to mail out a number of articles quickly. As far as I know, he hasn't gone any farther with this, but his approach sounds like the best one I've heard.

In class I have had inconsistent results in trying to make multi-sales to newspapers. Some students do well, others send out as many as eighty articles and make no sales.

WORKING THE NEWSPAPER MARKETS

From these experiences, I have put together a few rules that seem to work well.

1. *Study the newspapers to see what kinds of articles they are taking and how they want these articles put together.* Keep in mind that these features must appeal to a very general audience. Clip out a few features as models and construct yours the same way. Keep the length to about 1,100 words or less.

2. *Make up your own newspaper list from either* Editor and Publisher International Year Book, Bacons Publicity Checker *or* Standard Rate and Data. All are available in most libraries.

3. *Divide this list as George Beinhorn did so that you have separate listings for the statewide, regional, and smaller newspapers.*

4. *Mail to about thirty to thirty-five statewide newspapers the first year for each article.* The second year mail to all the regionals and so forth.

So far we haven't decided whether it's best to address these articles to "feature editor" at each newspaper or to address each individual feature editor by name. I personally feel you can make more sales by going directly to an individual editor. I have had students do well, however, by simply using the generic "feature editor." You will need to experiment to find which works best for you.

This again is the same article, simply resold "as is" without reslanting. We print up a hundred or so of any one article at a quick print service for about thirty-five dollars and mail them out without return postage. (We don't care whether the article is returned by the newspaper or not.) If we need more, we just have them printed.

See figure 7-1 for the first page set up. Write "Exclusive to your circulation area" in the right-hand corner. In the upper left-hand corner put the word and symbol "copyright ©," your name, and "one time rights." By the way, the minute you write something, you then own common-law copyright. You do not need to register your work with the copyright office to have legal copyright on your own work.

```
Copyright  ©  1988                    Exclusive to Your
Duane Newcomb                         Circulation Area
708 Fourth St.
Anytime, CA 95999
one time rights




          SIERRA WRITING CAMP HELPS WRITERS EARN FAME AND FORTUNE

     Grass Valley, California
          It's not surprising to find summer camps today offering
     everything from computers to performing arts, but very few can
     boast that their campers, using the skills learned at camp, have
     gone on to earn a name for themselves in the literary world.
          Since its inception in 1975 Sierra Writing Camp students
     have sold several hundred books, both fiction and non-fiction,
     and thousands of articles.  Camper Phyllis Halldorson of
     Sacramento California first began selling confession stories.
     Then went on to publish such romance novels as "Temporary Bride"
     and "If I Ever Love You."  Shirley Parenteau, who attended camp
     the first three years, published eight children's books and two
     Ballantine romances.  John and Valerie Thompson co-authored
     an illustrated book about hot tubs for Chronicle Books called
```

Figure 7-1.   Syndicated newspaper feature. Place your name and address in the left hand corner. Write "exclusive your circulation area" in the right hand corner. This lets the feature editor know that you will not sell the same feature to competing newspapers, but will be offering the article beyond their circulation area.

JUVENILE RELIGIOUS MAGAZINES

This group represents a good market for articles on subjects like hobbies, handicraft, nature, outdoor activities, science, crafts, sports, bike riding, pets, and personal experiences. The reason they are willing to buy second (reprint) rights is that the readers of Presbyterian magazines don't read Methodist magazines, the readers of Methodist magazines don't read Catholic magazines, and so forth.

Some of the magazines that will take simultaneous and previously published submissions are *Action, Counselor, Crusader Magazine, Dash, Nature Friend Magazine, Our Little Friend, Primary Treasure, Story Friends, Touch,* and the *Young Crusader.* The markets here are low paying, sometimes in the two- to three-cent-a-word range, but you can usually sell each article several times.

Over the years, my classes have sold a number of articles in this field. Several years ago one of my students gathered up her own and several neighbor children and drove up to Lick Observatory near San Jose, California, where they were given a guided tour. My student took pictures of the kids looking through one of the telescopes, being shown pictures of the stars, walking up the outside steps, and other details. She also took some establishing shots of the interior and exterior of the observatory. When she returned home she wrote a very simple 800-word story entitled "Visit to an Observatory." The result: eight sales for a total of about $300.

Juvenile religious magazines are listed in *Writer's Market,* the *Religious Writer's Marketplace,* and Sally Stuart's *Christian Writer.* See the Bibliography for the addresses.

MULTISUBMISSION BASICS

If you want to try writing for this field, always send for sample copies of all the magazines listed. Study each magazine carefully; then decide what topic you know about that several publications might be interested in.

Again, you will be reselling the same article to each magazine. You will, however, need two to five pictures for each article. The same pictures are sent to each magazine.

It has been my experience in over twenty years of full-time freelancing that at least eighty percent of all juvenile freelance articles require either photographs or illustrations. I suggest you send the manuscript, without querying, to all possible markets, and tell the editor that photographs or illustrations are available. This way you will avoid the expense of printing twenty to forty photos or the effort of putting together a number of drawings, without knowing whether or not you will make the sale.

Set up the first page of the manuscript here exactly as we did for newspaper features. But in the right-hand corner, instead of writing "exclusive to your circulation area," say "simultaneous submission."

RULE OF THUMB

If you look in the juvenile listings in *Writer's Market,* you will find that many of these publications say that simultaneous submission is okay. With many of the five areas discussed in this chapter, however, the magazine's listing will not indicate that they take articles sold to other magazines. The only way you can find out is to try.

What I do as a rule of thumb is look for magazines that do not compete with each other, and clearly state on the manuscript what I am doing. After that the editor can decide whether he wants to accept multisubmission or not. In practice, I find that doing things this way is quite acceptable.

CITY AND REGIONAL MAGAZINES

City and regional magazines are probably one of the fastest growing of all magazine categories. A few years ago only about fifteen of these publications existed. Today there are 147 and the end of the growth spurt doesn't appear to be in sight.

Titles in this category include *San Diego, Los Angeles, Texas Monthly, Washington, Utah Holiday, Palm Beach Life, Twin Cities,* and more. Some focus on city life, others specialize in business, home, garden, and sports.

"The city magazine," says Ed Prizer, publisher of *Orlando*, "is, in effect, a magazine for newcomers. It is the new, young, mobile blood that is coming into the community for whom the city magazines serve a definite service role. The great success of city magazines is in communities in which there is a heavy immigration of upscale persons."

As a result, many of these magazines offer an editorial mix of restaurant reviews, guides to local night life, lifestyle and service features, plus a wide range of articles slanted toward an upscale reader.

REGIONAL SLANT

Here are some samples of articles from selected issues of *Los Angeles,* and *Utah Holiday:* "A Train Lover's Tour Through Downtown Los Angeles," "Jazz Legends That Live in Los Angeles," "Joe Sam Chronicles the Life and Times of the Black Cowboy," and "Utah's Strange Case of Parental Kidnapping."

A few of these magazines also run a number of investigative articles. Ron Javers, editor of *Philadelphia,* believes that investigative journalism should be a crucial part of a magazine's editorial mix. As a result, *Philadelphia* has reported on topics as varied as organized crime and the search for fugitive financier Robert Vesco. *Milwaukee* reported on the politics of cable TV franchising and the manipulation of tax money by their city hall. Others have handled similar hard-hitting stories.

WHAT TO SUBMIT

For the most part, city and regional magazines run fairly sophisticated articles with a local angle. If this is true, how can a writer hope to sell a story to more than one of these publications at a time? The answer lies in the fact that these publications cater to an upscale audience intensely interested in a full, rich life.

As a result, many run, in addition to their regular features, general articles on gardening, food, taxes, jobs, organizing your closets, updating your wardrobe, shopping, managing your time, divorce, marriage, and personal relationships. Some also feature quizzes such as "Rate Your Sex Drive," and "What is Your Creativity Quotient?"

It is true that these general articles represent only a small percentage of each magazine's total editorial content, but collectively they offer a significant market for multiple sales of the same article.

You will find the most complete listing of these magazines in the *Standard Rate and Data, Consumer Edition,* available in most libraries. Begin by sending for copies of as many of these magazines as possible.

MAKE A LIST

I suggest that you make a complete list of all the general articles you find. This will give you a good idea of what you can do. You can query each publication if you like. But most general articles are fairly short. Simply make as many copies of your article as you need and send them to every possible market.

NONCOMPETITIVE PUBLICATIONS

Sometimes when you sell an article to one magazine, you can turn around and sell the same article (second rights) to magazines that are noncompetitive with the original publication. Many times you must reslant it to make additional sales. See chapter 2.

But some articles such as a short piece on "How Creative Are You?" "Are You Compatible With Your Mate?" and similar general features can be submitted to several different fields at once without change.

I suggest you go back through *Writer's Market,* as we did in chapter 2, and see how many additional possibilities you can find. Make up a number of copies at a quick-print shop, and send out a copy, without query, to any possible market. This again is the same article, not a reslant. What you want to sell here is "second serial rights." I simply mark this "second rights" after my name and address and copyright in the left hand corner.

Besides this, keep looking for new markets or markets you might have missed. To find these, I regularly go through the market announcements in *Writer's Digest* to see if I can turn up any new publications that look promising. I also thumb through the magazines on the newsstands to look for possibilities. I even go through magazines at the dentist's office. Be diligent and keep searching; you'll be surprised how many additional sales you will make.

THE GLOBAL MARKET

Worldwide, there are some 70,000 magazines published in forty nations where you can sell the same article ten to forty times for a total price of between $2,000 and $20,000. This creates a far different article marketplace than just the United States alone. In the future, the main market for freelancers may well be the entire globe and not one particular nation.

WHAT KIND OF MAGAZINES

Worldwide you will find magazines published in virtually the same categories as they are in the United States: general magazines, women's, men's, science, automotive, trade/business, Sunday newspaper publishers, corporate, and organization/association magazines. These are listed in Ulrich's *International Periodicals Directory*, and Europa Yearbook. *Ulrich's* is essential for freelancers, and you will find it in most libraries.

WHAT IS A GLOBAL ARTICLE? In simplest terms, a global article is one that will interest readers worldwide. An article about an American businesswoman who started a successful novelty pillow business in her garage probably would not be of interest around the world because few of the world's readers would relate to this. But an article on genetic engineering and how it is changing the world's crops, along with the impact this may make on the world's food supply, probably is.

The leading freelance practitioner in this field is James Joseph of Southern California. If you are serious about becoming an expert in global marketing, you might consider purchasing Joseph's tapes and workbook on the global writer's market. The address is *Writer's World*, P.O. Box 24678, Los Angeles, CA 90024.

Joseph has sold numerous articles throughout the world. Here are some of the titles he finds to be of worldwide interest.

"Only Robots Will Apply: How Robots Will Soon Steal Your Job." With robots appearing in factories worldwide, you can see why this would be of interest to the world's workers who wonder what's going to happen to their jobs when robots take over.

"Man-Powering The Channel: The Flight of Gossamer Albatross" (the bicycle-powered airplane). How it was built and what went into the cross-channel bicycle-powered airplane flight. This was an extremely popular article that appeared in many magazines worldwide.

"Bass Madness: Who Will Catch the U.S. $1 Million Bass?" There is bass fishing only in the United States, but the fact that it is the most popular type of fishing here and that there is a $1 million prize makes it a global piece.

"Get Away Now: Everybody's Passport to Space." This article tells how to get aboard a future shuttle flight.

QUERYING THE GLOBAL MARKET A global query is simply a standard query that (1) hooks the editor, (2) explains what the article will be about, (3) details what you are offering: the article, color photos, maps or graphics, and special sidebars, and (4) asks for the order. (See figure 7-2.) The query is sent out to as many markets as you feel might be interested.

WRITING THE GLOBAL ARTICLE All articles are written in English and will be translated by the magazine. Since the translation won't be in your style, keep the writing extremely simple and the sentences fairly short. In addition, you need to remove anything which would Americanize the piece, such as a reference to a well-known football player, or a slang term popular only in America.

Global articles can often be slanted to fit a number of markets by including one or more sidebars. An article about how genetic engineering is changing the world crops may be made suitable for the women's market by using a sidebar on a woman scientist who is a leading pioneer in the field. It might be turned into a business

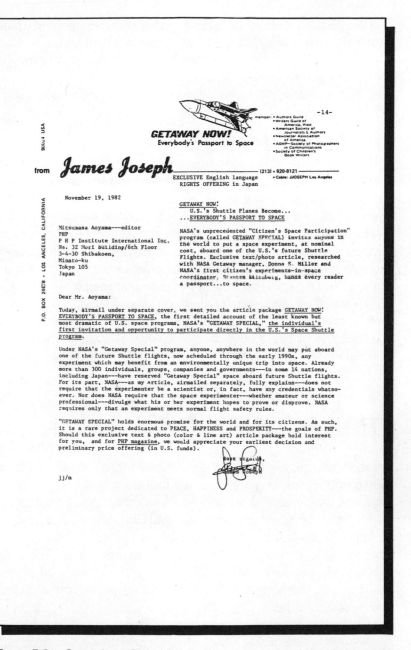

Figure 7-2.   Query for a Global Article. These articles can be sold country by country by offering the exclusive rights for that particular country. This one offers the English language rights in Japan.

article with a sidebar on the business opportunities opening up because of the new genetically altered crops.

Articles can be sold to magazines in each country by offering the exclusive rights for that particular country. If there are several languages in a country, as there are, for instance, in India, you can offer the exclusive rights to a particular language in that country.

THE TOTAL PACKAGE

When you receive a go-ahead, the total package you send should include the manuscript, six to twelve transparencies, sidebars, perhaps art, cover letter, an envelope, and coupons or a check for return postage.

The standard way of including return postage is to purchase international mailing coupons at the post office. James Joseph, however, always includes his personal check for the exact amount of the return postage instead of international coupons. The post office can tell you how much this will be. Joseph says, "Most of the time when you do this, the magazine will simply send your package back and not cash your check." Over a year's time this results in considerable savings.

TRADE JOURNALS

Trade journals are magazines published for readers in a wide variety of industries. In general, you'll find trade journals for manufacturers, wholesalers, and retailers. A number are also published for individual professions, such as medicine, law and education.

Approximately 4,500 trade journals are listed in the *Standard Rate and Data* business edition, available in most libraries. The listings contain the name of the magazine; the address and phone number; and the names of the editor, publisher, advertising sales manager, and others.

Usually the listing contains a statement of the policy, which includes who the magazine is published for and the editorial content: news, product information, merchandising, and so forth.

CREATING AN INVENTORY

Because I owned a retail store, I have expertise in advertising and merchandising. For years I wrote dealer articles. That is, articles about how one retailer did something especially well.

One of these stories told how a paint retailer established a rental art gallery within the store to attract foot traffic. Another explained how a feed and farm store did an exceptionally good job with on-shelf merchandising. All in all, I probably wrote two thousand or more of these articles over a ten-year period.

I became so efficient at this that I could start at one end of a shopping center, visit every store in the center, take pictures, interview the owners or managers, and come out at the other end with ten or fifteen articles and picture shorts that some magazine would buy. I would then put these pieces on tape while driving, drop them off at my typist on the way home, and send them off to the magazines the next day.

I dropped out of this field for several years to write books. Then about four years ago I decided that there might be a good opportunity here to write in-depth merchandising pieces that dealt with contemporary problems facing retailers.

As a result, I made up a list of two hundred retail-oriented magazines that will take either merchandising or advertising articles. These include such publications as *Yarn Market News, Jobber Topics, National Jeweler,* and *Fishing Tackle Trade News.* I am able to sell the same article here a number of times because the readers of jewelry magazines usually don't read toy magazines and these readers generally don't read retail photography magazines.

I then created what I call my inventory, a list of well-researched merchandising, advertising, and demographic articles. The titles on my first list included the following:

"Merchandising for Today's Great Decade of Change." This article details the tremendous changes taking place today that affect retailing: couples marrying later, working women, two-income families, more people working at home, the overall changing demographic picture, and several dozen other major changes. It also explains how the retailers can use these changes to keep their business up with and ahead of the times.

"The Advertising Workshop."   This article explains why retailers waste at least a portion of their advertising with ineffective ads placed in the wrong media. It also helps retailers plan and execute each stage of their ad campaigns in newspapers, television, radio, and the yellow pages.

"Sharpen Sales Skills with Communication Sales Training."   This article details a sales program developed by behavioral scientist Thomas Knutson, Ph.D., and shows how to approach retail sales in five basic steps (1) the approach, (2) the search for customers' needs, (3) the presentation of merchandise, (4) the request for action, and (5) the response to customer resistance.

Other titles in this series include "Creating a Selling Image for Your Business," "Tapping the Moving Market," "Target Marketing for the Retailer," and "Creative Outdoor Advertising."

THE MAKING OF AN ARTICLE

For most of these articles, I rely on a combination of research reports, interviews with industry leaders, and anything else I can find. Many take three or four months to put together. These trade journal articles don't bring much individually, only $225 each, but if I can sell $1,500 to $4,000 worth of articles on any one subject, I can justify the extensive research.

One of my most popular "self-syndicated" articles has been "Merchandising to the Working Woman." I started this piece by reading a number of magazines and clipping anything that related to the working woman. I found a great deal on this subject in *U.S. News and World Report, Ad Age,* and the *Los Angeles Times.* Using this as a starting place, I sent for all of the reports and studies these and other magazines mentioned. The US Labor Department had compiled statistics on the subject. Pollster Louis Harris issued a poll on working women, and *American Demographics* ran a number of articles on the subject that were loaded with statistics. There were also many others.

I then started calling about twenty authorities mentioned in these sources to do interviews; these included marketing consultants, advertising executives, and several university professors.

One of my most interesting interviews was with Dorothy Pollock, President of Vassarette (a major intimate apparel firm). She returned my call on a Saturday a few hours after returning from a fashion trip to Europe. I told her what I wanted and the next two hours she talked about the needs of the working woman. She also mailed me a fascinating study by *Glamour* magazine called the "Pyschology of Fashion," which detailed women's shopping motivation and the changes in their spending patterns. When I finished this research, I had enough to write a book on the subject. So far, the finished article has earned about $4,000.

MERCHANDISING THE SYNDICATED TRADE ARTICLE

I have two ways of merchandising these articles. I print what I call a "Business Editor's Article Hot List." This is a two-sided, 8½-by-11-inch page listing all of my available articles. (See figure 7-3.) I give a title and a one- or two-sentence description of each article. My first year's offerings featured eleven articles. Currently I offer forty-four articles a year printed on an eleven-by-seventeen-inch sheet.

I mail the "Hot List" to about 250 retail trade journal editors in February of each year. Along with this "Hot List," I include a cover letter and an order form. The cover letter states the price of the article, $225. For $100 more I will interview five to ten retailers in the magazine's field and work this back into the article. Eventually, I intend to also offer a graphics option for another $100.

The order form has a place for the editor to list the article number, the name of the article, and the date they need the piece. I now have editors who order four to six articles at a time. From the entire "Hot List" last year I received forty-seven orders for articles.

In addition to this, I make up a multiple query that lists two or sometimes three articles. I mail these every other month to my entire mailing list, which is handled by computer. Every letter has an individualized heading for each editor. This bi-monthly mailing usually adds another seven to twenty assignments per mailing.

1986

Business Editor's

ARTICLE HOT LIST

ADVERTISING/PROMOTION

128 - TV ADVERTISING . . . Are you Overlooking a Good Bet?: Although rates have risen astronomically the last few years, this media still offers a tremendous opportunity. This article explains how to evaluate your market, details the do's and don'ts of ad planning, evaluates the rate ratio and provides a media glossary.

129 - HOW TO GET FREE ADVERTISING FROM YOUR LOCAL NEWSPAPER: You can easily double and triple your advertising effectiveness by taking advantage of free newspaper publicity. Local newspapers regularly run hundreds of news items each year on or about business activities, community involvement, openings, alterations, awards and other events. This article explains how to create news, submit it to the local newspapers and couple news releases with advertising to keep your business constantly in the public eye.

130 - MINING THE FULL POTENTIAL OF CO-OP ADVERTISING: Co-op advertising offers the retailer a double edge sword for increasing the effectiveness of his or her advertising program. This article explains the various plans, shows how to obtain co-op funds in all media including cable television, details what kind of co-op is available (from ad mats to television commercials with dealer tags) and explains how to obtain a complete listing of all current manufacturer (over 2000) co-op plans.

131 - CABLE TELEVISION . . . Will it Work for You?: Cable television is undoubtedly the best buy in advertising today. It reaches target audiences better than any other media, delivers your customers without waste and is the least expensive of all major media. This article explains the in's and out's of cable television for the retailer, details how to start, how to obtain co-op for cable and how to measure results.

137 - CREATIVE OUTDOOR ADVERTISING: Currently outdoor advertising, a billion dollar a year business is healthy, growing, provocative and more creative than ever. Currently the biggest new trend in outdoor advertising is co-op between retailers and national marketers in fields ranging from photo dealers to Western wear retailers to furniture and other areas. This article explains the new trends and shows how to use outdoor advertising effectively to compliment your other merchandising efforts.

142 - THE ADVERTISING WORKSHOP: Many retailers waste at least a portion of every advertising dollar with ineffective ads placed in the wrong media. This article explains how to plan and execute each stage of your ad program to obtain maximum results for every dollar spent.

143 - RX FOR YOUR NEWSPAPER ADVERTISING: The Newspaper Advertising Bureau finds that the most successful ads are those which have a distinctive look and instantly telegraph your message. In addition a Million Market Newspapers Inc. study finds that ad positioning and timing make a difference: ads must be placed in the section that best reaches your target market. This article details what makes a good newspaper ad and provides a checklist with which to compare your present newspaper advertising.

144 - PUT SELL POWER IN YOUR YELLOW PAGES AD: A recent study by Statistical Research, Inc. found that Americans turn to the Yellow Pages more than 43 million times each day. Writing a good yellow pages ad involves answering the key questions of Who? ... What? ... Where? ... When? ... and Why? This article explains how to design an effective ad, build a good logo, and write attention getting copy.

145 - CLASSIFIED ADS ... BIG CLOUT ON A SMALL BUDGET: Retailers, according to the Newspaper Advertising Bureau, currently sell $50 billion or more worth of merchandise each year through ads placed in the classified sections. Many retailers, however, need help in making their classifieds more effective. This article offers a four step formula for writing effective classified ads and shows how to make them an important part of your advertising program.

147 - POINT OF PURCHASE ADVERTISING: Good point of purchase P-O-P advertising increases sales without requiring additional advertising budget, or sales help. This article shows how to get the most out of your P-O-P by selecting the right merchandise, by tying it to other advertising, by using attention getters by proper positioning and by backing P-O-P displays with silent salesman signs.

BUSINESS EDITOR'S ARTICLE HOT LIST:
Data Base Articles — A Trade Industry First

This hot list features topical business articles available from Duane Newcomb Editorial Services. A pre-researched computer data base for each article has been put together from interviews with national authorities, surveys and industry reports. When the order is received each article is computer-tailored for each field and each magazine. Each can be farther customized with telephone interviews with individual businesses within your field. Articles can be ordered on the enclosed form and delivered as a conventional manuscript, a computer diskette, or by modem directly to your computer.

Duane Newcomb Editorial Services, 18293 Crystal St., Grass Valley, CA 95945. (916) 272-8047

Figure 7-3.   Multiple query for syndicated trade journal articles. This pamphlet is actually a printed query that lists a number of articles. Editors are encouraged to order by number.

WRITING THE ARTICLE

When I write my original article, I make up a data base on a computer disk. That is, I write the article in a general way, referring to the reader as "retailer." I also indicate six or seven places where this particular article could be changed to tailor it to a certain readership. This is not reslanting.

The article itself basically remains the same. I simply insert material which makes it of greater interest to say, photo retailers, toy dealers, bicycle dealers, or whatever audience I'm writing for.

When I receive an order from a particular magazine like *Professional Furniture Retailer,* I copy the general article (called a "model") to another file to write the final article.

I then make the changes I need to tailor the piece to the *Professional Furniture Retailer.* There is a place in the working woman's article, for instance, where I list some women's shopping preferences in furniture for style, color, and upholstery fabric, plus some other general information. Here is the insert:

"Working women are extremely fashion oriented and are at home with contemporary styles and colors. They also are fabric conscious, preferring velvet, jacquard/textured/woven, nylon and cotton in that order (this refers to furniture upholstery).

"The Congress Office of Technology Assessment shows that more working couples are finding their entertainment at home. This means greater opportunity for entertainment and wall furniture. For working women, the master bedroom also is rapidly becoming a place to relax after the work day. As a result, many women are adding upholstered chairs, occasional tables, recliners, desks and electronic wall units to the bedroom furnishings."

When I'm finished, the article fits the magazine well. And it's even better if I insert retailer interviews. The market for these articles, I find, is getting stronger all the time. While I use a computer to tailor the articles, they can be written on a typewriter using the "cut and paste" system. That is, you simply type up the inserts on a separate sheet of paper, cut them apart and paste them in where you need them. When you finish, don't retype; simply photocopy the article with the inserts in place.

Is it possible to sell one article many times? Of course it is. I suggest you go back through your files and look for article ideas that can be sold to newspapers, the juvenile market, regional magazines, secondary magazines, or the global market. You may be surprised to find that you have already written articles you can resell for an additional $200 to $4,000. Trade journal pieces, of course, need to be written as originals, then resold to a number of magazines. The overall market, for all fields, is a big one that every writer should tap for as many additional sales as possible.

8. How to Make an Article Data Bank Work for You

An article data bank is simply a reservoir of material built up as you go about your business of writing articles. It consists of interviews conducted for previously published articles, all of your research materials, and the articles themselves. If you handle this data bank right, you should be able to use the information it contains to create many more articles and even books.

Years ago when I interviewed Erle Stanley Gardner for an article, he spent more than an hour talking to me about writing. One piece of advice he gave me at the time was to always "use the interest of your writing, never the principal." I puzzled over this for a long time. But then I realized that what he actually meant was that the material you generate, the interviews you conduct, the facts you gather, and the pictures you take are your "principal."

If you use this information once and stop, you are using up that "principal." But if you spin off a number of articles from the material you've gathered, then you are collecting the "interest" for your efforts.

Gardner himself did this well when he used the same characters over and over again in his Perry Mason series. He repeated this same process when he invented the Bertha Cool and Donald Lam characters for another series. But Gardner went further than this. Every time he did anything, it turned up later in his writing. I discovered this firsthand when five months after I interviewed him, the details of our meeting appeared in one of his books on houseboating on the California Delta. Time and time again, some of the material he collected writing one book would appear again and again in his other books.

If you intend to sell as much of your writing as you possibly can, you must learn to do this. Here are some methods that work well.

BUILD FROM PROJECTS YOU'VE ALREADY COMPLETED

Once you've sold an article, don't quit looking for ways to sell the material contained in that article in other, sometimes unrelated ways. I wrote several general houseboating articles in which I surveyed the houseboating manufacturers and described the various models. Part of the material I collected concerned small trailable houseboats, boats that could be lived in at a campground and also could be moved easily from one body of water to another.

I managed to sell one article to a camping magazine. I then turned this around and sold a roundup on the same subject to *Better Homes and Gardens.* When I finished this, I proposed a book on houseboating using this same information and some additional material from the files. Prentice Hall brought it out under the title *The Wonderful World of Houseboating.*

I know a retired game warden who wrote one article on his experiences as a game warden. Then, building on this experience, he wrote a piece on abalone poaching. Then he took some of the funnier things that happened when he was a warden and sold "Silly Excuses Game Violators Use" to *Field and Stream.*

MINE THE FULL POTENTIAL

Here are two questions I ask myself when looking over my articles.

What parts of this manuscript might be used as a basis for additional articles?   When writing gardening articles, I included some material on drip watering. I decided this could certainly be used somewhere. As a result, I sold this material to several gardening magazines.

In answering this question, go over your manuscript carefully and look for even insignificant items. Sometimes you might simply touch on something in your manuscript that can be expanded into another article with just a little more digging. A mention of an expert on local baseball lore might be developed into a regional personality piece. A paragraph or two on tune-ups in an article on automobile care could be expanded into an informative article on tune-ups alone.

How many additional markets can I find for this material?   I simply run this through the system suggested in chapter 2 using *Writer's Market*. If I can come up with five or more possible markets, I start to work immediately.

WORK IN RELATED FIELDS

If you write a travel article, then a religious article, then one on children, nothing will tie together and you'll have to start new to research every piece.

If you work in related fields, however, quite often when you write an article for one field, it will automatically fit somewhere else. A good example of this is trailers, campers, motor homes, the outdoors and camping, and even outdoor sports. In building my writing business, I try to keep my fields all tied together so I can cut down my research effort.

This goes far beyond specialization. If you do not select a particular specialty, you will find that it pays to tie your broad writing interests together. If you select a specialty, you should keep related interests within the specialty together. I consider this extremely important.

As I mentioned, I write a lot of articles for retail trade business magazines. This includes the following fields: drugs, sporting goods, luggage and leather goods, automotive, lawn and garden, the shooting industry, and furniture.

The common denominator here is merchandising, so a general article for one has the potential of selling to all of the others. I might sell an article on a certain sales system to several magazines.

The same is true of gardening. I might write something for a woman's magazine on how to decorate with vegetables, write about how to pick out showy vegetables for a garden magazine, and then turn out a specialized piece on cooking with baby vegetables for a gourmet magazine. All of these could be derived from basically the same material.

TAP THE FULL POTENTIAL OF ALL INTERVIEWS

Let's say you're interviewing a local personality for a regional magazine. You discover, in conversation, that this particular individual uses an RV as a traveling office, owns a dune buggy (which he uses to explore Baja, California in the winter and spring), has taken his trailable houseboat to Alaska, and skin dives.

You can then turn these interests into articles for the magazines within these fields. I recently interviewed a university professor who had developed a sales training method for retailers based on behavioral psychology. This article, as I mentioned in chapter 7, sold to a number of trade business magazines. During the interview the professor mentioned that he was also beginning to use behavioral psychology in the retailers' war against shoplifting. Here was an entirely new article I could develop and sell, based on the same principle.

INFORMATION BASICS   How do you set up your interviews to get the greatest yield of information? Sometimes I expand the interview to include as many areas as possible. When I finish I have almost enough for several pieces. If not, I call back for additional details. Sometimes I simply make a notation about the possibilities. Other times, when I go through my notes or transcribed tapes, I look for something, almost anything, that might make another article. If this looks promising, I'll probably call back and do another complete interview on the phone. More than once, I have turned up three or four articles this way when I thought I had only one.

ROUNDUPS

Roundup articles provide a place to tap the material you have already collected, gathering it into an overview of "ten best . . ." or "three ways to . . ." or "new developments in. . . ." Several years ago I wrote a number of articles on individual outdoor restaurants that could be reached by boat. Each article covered a single restaurant.

When I finished the series of nine, I took the recipes and some of the information from each article and rounded them up into a piece entitled, "Cooking Tips from Waterfront Restaurants."

Several years ago I wrote a number of travel articles for *Trailer Life* magazine. Later I spun the information off into "Ten Hot Spots for RV Travel on the West Coast."

Maybe you have written articles on resorts that make a big production out of the Christmas holidays. One of these I have covered several times is the Ahwahnee Hotel in Yosemite National Park. This old hotel goes all-out at Christmas time and has become so popular that you have to book reservations far in advance.

If you have a number of these, you might round them up into "Five Great Spots for a Christmas Vacation." Or perhaps you have written some in-depth pieces on particular methods or systems for giving up smoking. These might become "Ten Tips to Help You Quit Smoking."

Periodically review the articles you have written to see if they offer roundup possibilities.

UPDATES

Articles you have already sold can often be updated and resold to a number of markets. Always keep an eye open for a new peg or a twist that will add to the piece's salability. Recent national recognition of a university professor by some organization, for instance, will make your article on that individual even more salable than when you first wrote it.

Or say you wrote but couldn't sell an article on a research team that has created (through gene splicing) a number of specially adapted crops. Then a year later a congressional committee starts to investigate gene splicing and focuses national attention on its uses in agriculture. This attention will give your article new life.

Anniversary dates also increase your chances with any update. Disneyland's thirtieth and fortieth birthdays offer you a chance to update and refocus attention on this travel attraction. If you have a few pieces in your files about the pioneer residents of a certain city and that city is about to celebrate its fiftieth, hundredth, or two hundredth year, pull those pieces out of the files, tie them into the anniversary, and send them on their way.

BASICS FOR MARKETING UPDATES   Be sure, also, that you offer your update back to the magazine that published it originally. One of my articles on mobile home living was updated and sold to the same retirement magazine three times; the editor felt that after about a four-year period his readers were ready for the same subject.

Most magazines repeat subjects on a cyclical basis. Some find that their readership has changed considerably during this period so the subject is really not redundant to the current readership.

Because of this, I always make it a point to first ask the magazine that originally published the piece (in a query letter) if they want to do an update. If they don't, I then query other magazines I feel might be interested.

This update query letter should (1) explain when the article was first published, (2) emphasize the new developments that have taken place, and (3) detail how you intend to handle the updated piece.

HOW TO UPDATE   Updating an article is a fairly simple process. Here are the steps:

1. *Continue to research.* When you write and sell an article, don't simply file it away and forget it. Continue to clip material on this subject from newspapers and magazines. That way you will have current information in your files when you are ready to update.

In the future, I probably will not do nearly as much clipping as I do now. I intend to use one of the computer services to dig out all articles in the major newspapers and magazines that have been written on the subject since the original article was published. This will not only save me a lot of work, it will be far more complete. After all, I can't keep track of every article published in the *New York Times,* the *Christian Science Monitor,* the *Wall Street Journal,* and other publications. But the commercial data bases can certainly do so.

When does it become feasible to subscribe to one of the services? That depends on you. If you do not already own a computer, you first have to decide when you can afford to buy one. I personally believe that anyone serious about selling articles needs to make a computer one of his or her first purchases.

After that, it depends on how much you do. My rule of thumb is that it is feasible to subscribe to one of the more inexpensive data bases (see page 167) when you are selling five to six articles a year that take extensive research. I suggest that you send for the information from several of the services, add up the cost, and see if you feel they might be worthwhile. Not only should you consider the primary expense, however, but also the amount of time you would have to invest handling your research the conventional way.

2. *Make sure your statistics are current.* When you decide to update, go through your article and look for all statistical references. In an article on shoplifting, you might, for instance, have included information on the number of shoplifting cases or convictions that occurred in a particular year. In a travel article, you might have referred to the population of a town, state, or country. Statistical information needs updating for the current year. You can often do this by calling the library for the information or by putting in a phone call to the public information office of a government agency. See chapter 5 for more information on research.

3. *Update the quotes.* The persons quoted in your original article may now have different things to say about the subject. Some individuals may no longer be in the field, may have changed jobs, or may have died. Call or write each of them, explain the quote you used before and ask them if they would like to update it or have additional information on the subject.

If you have included, in your original article or notes, the name of the person, the city, and the institution or business they represented, you should be able to find them easily through your telephone information operator. If their number is unlisted, you might try phoning them at work. Or write. University authorities can be reached through the university's public relations office.

4. *Include any new developments.* Often when a year or two have gone by, you will find a number of changes within the general field that should be included in your article. In one case I wrote an article on recreational vehicles, which I updated four years later. When I first wrote the article, fifth wheel trailers were not very important. When I did the update, however, they represented an important option for anyone interested in RVs. To make the article complete, I had to include this information.

5. *Consider shifting the emphasis.* If you are rewriting this piece for the magazine you sold the article to originally, you will want to make some changes in emphasis or in the overall construction of the article. If, for instance, your original article was a travel piece on the Pacific Northwest, you might consider shifting the emphasis in the update slightly to something like "Ten Must-See Attractions of the Pacific Northwest."

This article would include much of the same information as the original, but would focus on ten specific attractions instead of regional areas. It isn't always necessary to shift emphasis, but it's worth considering since it helps add an extra dimension to your original article.

LET YOUR RESEARCH SUGGEST OTHER POSSIBILITIES

Every time you research an article, you always turn up more material than you can ever use in the article itself. In doing an article called "The Underground Shopper," I turned up a lot of material on how to shop the supermarket more efficiently, where to buy mail-order goods at wholesale, how to keep out of bankruptcy, how to cut medical and automotive expenses, and how to shop for a home loan. I turned this information into a series of articles that have sold again and again.

When you finish writing your original articles, make it a practice to go back through your research material and try to come up with as many ideas as possible for additional pieces. In doing this, I generally search through my notes and other materials several times. This helps me turn up every possible idea that I might find there.

BOOKS FROM ARTICLES

Sometimes when you write a series of articles on the same subject, you can later put all of them together as a book. In one case, I had written a number of gardening articles that were slanted especially to people living in mobile homes. The problem on a mobile home lot is that the garden must be designed to fit into a small space. I sold these to several trailer magazines and a retirement magazine.

After I had written about thirty of them, I put together a proposal and approached a publisher who specialized in RVs and mobile home living. The result: a book called *The Mobile Home Gardening Guide*. This book remained on the publisher's list for about twelve years and returned about a thousand dollars a year during that time.

A friend of mine who writes a column about service life for an armed services newspaper recently suggested a collection of her columns as a possible book. As a result, she was offered a contract by Stackpole Books.

How can you do this? Ask yourself:

Do I have a series of articles that might be book material? This would be some series with a unified theme. A group of articles on "How to Cook Italian" might well make a good book on Italian cooking. A series of articles on "Understanding Auto Repair for Women," which discussed tune-ups, brakes, changing oil, meaningful noises to listen for, and other subjects could well make a book on *Easy Auto Repair for Women*.

Do these articles cover the full range of the subject or do I need additional research? The articles on Italian cooking, for instance, may well need to be filled out with more recipes. Or you might need to do a section on pasta or something similar.

What publishers would be interested in publishing this material as a book?   I suggest that you check the publishers listed in *Writer's Market*. Simply list the ones who take your subject. You might also look at the spring and fall announcement issues of *Publisher's Weekly*. These issues include publishers' listings of books.

To approach publishers you will need a query letter (letter of inquiry), a proposal, an outline, and a couple of sample chapters (in some cases you can use the articles as chapters). A book query letter is written just like a magazine query letter, except instead of asking for the assignment, you offer to send any interested publisher the proposal, outline, and sample chapters. For details on how to write these, consult *How to Write a Book Proposal* by Michael Larsen.

Generally, I send the query letter to every publisher on the list. If I get several publishers who want to see the additional material, I photocopy this and send it to every publisher at once.

In my book classes I have found that if you send out twenty-five to thirty queries with a top-notch subject, you usually find five to seven publishers who want to see the sample material. Out of this number we sometimes get one offer of a contract, maybe two. When we receive the first offer, we contact all the other publishers still looking at the material, tell them we have an offer for so much money, and ask them, if they are interested in also making an offer, to please do it by a date we specify.

In practice, I have found that we never get more than one additional offer. Sometimes this additional offer is for a little more than the advance stipulated by the first publisher, sometimes for the same amount. After that, it's simply a matter of selecting the one you like best.

HOW TO SELL REJECTED MATERIAL

Rejected material should also be considered as part of your data bank. Believe it or not, those articles that most of us put back in the files can often be pulled back out and sold. Here is a procedure I have used successfully for many years to sell rejected material.

Recheck your writing to make sure it is professional. Look at the beginning and ending, the organization, the theme or main subject, the mechanics of the article, the anecdotes, the statistics, the quotes, and the conformity of the article to the magazine's style. Use the checklist in chapter 6, page 123.

Watch for new developments. Let's say you wrote an article on the rash of false child molestation cases being filed against husbands by wives going through a divorce, who want to keep the husbands from getting custody of the children.

You have details about a number of cases. For example, the police broke into the husband's house in the middle of the night, handcuffed him, and took him off to jail, where he spent several months behind bars. After a long, drawn-out process, the man finally cleared himself in court.

Your article gets turned down by a number of magazines because: "The public's perception is that these cases are so horrible that anyone accused must be guilty." This was the response to an excellent article written by one of my students. The student withdrew it from circulation and filed it.

Since then a number of cases of deliberate false accusation have begun to surface. The newspapers have exposed this, and several stories about it have appeared on TV.

This is the point when my student should pull out the article and send it in again. The climate has changed, and maybe now, the editors will feel it is a believable story.

Look for an upswing in public interest. Any time the public becomes interested in a subject, the magazines will hop on the bandwagon. Articles on shopping for discount bargains were well-received in 1982 when the economy faltered. Four years later it was a different story. Consumers were again back chasing the latest fad to charge on their credit cards. This will change, and in a few years discount bargains will again be popular.

Perhaps you did an article a few years ago on grandmothers marching for peace. A few protests had been staged and a small but dedicated group marched along the streets protesting nuclear weapons. Since that time we have had the great peace march and the attention of the country has been focused on the disarmament question. Even Doctor Spock was arrested protesting nuclear production. The public's interest is focused back on this question. Now is the time to pull your article out and send it in.

Be alert for any change in the magazine's emphasis. Magazines, as already mentioned, frequently change emphasis and format. *Mother Jones* has long been famous for investigative articles. Recently, however, they decided their audience had switched emphasis and no longer wanted to read as much about the evils of atomic energy and similar subjects as they once did. As a result, you can now sell them more general pieces.

As I mentioned in chapter 4, the writers' magazines will frequently alert you to these changes. If you have rejected manuscripts that fit the new direction, by all means send them back the minute you become aware of what's happening.

Watch the letters to the editors. If you have written an article on how to walk your way to a healthy heart and the editor has turned it down, yet a few months later you notice a few letters from readers on walking, do you leave your manuscript in the file? Of course not! If the readers are starting to show an interest, the editor will probably be in the market for an article on walking as exercise. Send it back.

Look for a switch in editors. Any time an editor leaves, it becomes a new ball game. Many times an article will be rejected by one editor, but the next one will think that same piece is great.

This has happened to me more times than I care to remember. I once wrote an article for a well-known magazine. When the editor rejected it, he said he had lost the manuscript. I dropped him a short note to thank him, then I forgot about the piece. Much to my surprise, one day I received a letter from a new editor saying that one of the assistant editors found my article. He thought it would fit his new editorial policy and they would be running the piece in an upcoming issue.

In another case, I had written several articles for *American Bicyclist and Motorcyclist* that were published. They ordered three more but rejected them. Then a few months later I noticed a new editor's name on the masthead. I pulled all three pieces out of the file and sent them in. He purchased these immediately and asked for three more.

My attitude now is that *there is no such thing as a rejected article. It is just a manuscript that hasn't been sold yet.* I have also learned not to take a single editor's opinion very seriously. My motto here is a writer nearly always outlives an editor. That is, the writer is going to be around a long time, but a lot of editors aren't. And although one editor might not like your piece, the next one may think you're the best writer he's ever seen.

Be alert for changes in thinking among leaders in a field or industry. Any time the emphasis changes, you can sell articles that couldn't be sold before.

Currently the thinking about the artificial heart is that it has only limited application. But suppose some scientist develops one that solves most of the problems and receives the support of the scientific community. At that point, articles on artificial hearts and their possibilities for the future would be very much in demand.

These aren't all the changes that will affect the salability of your writing, but they are the major ones that will enable you to tell when to send back manuscripts that have made the rounds and just weren't taken at that particular time.

SIX WAYS TO KEEP YOUR FILES ACTIVE

Stay alert for new and different ways to resell your material. Here are six ways to do this:

Pull an article out of your files once a week and list all the possible markets. Writers often forget that their files contain salable material. By making a conscious effort to do this on a regular basis, you will force yourself to focus on the possibilities. I suggest you take each idea as you come to it in your files and run it through the marketing system described in chapter 2.

Schedule every published article to go out again in four years. Make a list of all possible non-competing markets. If you like, you can submit to all of these simultaneously. Be sure you resubmit to the publication that bought the piece in the first place.

Pick one magazine, then leaf through your files checking each of your articles for a possible sale. Sometimes I'll select a magazine like *Friendly Exchange,* which buys travel articles. Then I'll run through all my published travel articles one by one, asking myself, "Would the magazine be interested in this one?" I'm always surprised at the number of additional sales I make this way.

Circulate a printed query.   Sometimes pull four articles you think are especially good. Enlarge or reduce the most illustrative photograph from each article to 2¼-inch size and paste the four photos to an 8½-by-11-inch page. Write a sentence or two about each article and have the sentences typeset. Paste each one- or two-sentence description under the appropriate picture. Then have fifty copies printed at a quick printing service ($2.00 to $2.50). Send this out with a note and let the editors check off the articles they want. Some writers do very well using this system.

Schedule a file review once a year.   Take a week and do nothing but go through your files. Compare every article to your list of possible reprint markets. Don't try to second-guess an editor. If you think he or she might be at all interested, by all means, pull the article and send it out.

Occasionally have another writer look through your files. Ask that person to suggest other places to sell your material. Often he or she will see possibilities you missed and also may be able to suggest markets you may have overlooked.

Pick an article you think is good, then tell yourself you are not going to stop until you've made fifty to a hundred sales (pick a figure).   Go through every possible channel to market your article. During the next year, keep trying to push sales. Every time you pick up a magazine, ask yourself, "Is this a market?"

With special emphasis like this, you'll be surprised how many ways you'll find to resell your manuscripts. Each method may not seem important, but by spotlighting it and concentrating attention, it is possible to increase your overall sales.

It is important that you use your data bank as effectively as possible. I know that this works because for one entire year I supported my family by working my files, creating new articles out of material already there, finding markets for already sold manuscripts, and by selling almost ninety percent of my previously rejected articles. During that year's time I didn't attempt to research or write any outside articles.

What I can do, you can do, too. I hope, however, that you won't stop researching and creating brand new articles, but that you will consider the methods outlined in this chapter as an integral part of your overall writing operation. They will help you obtain a far greater return from your writing than you could any other way.

TO THE READER

Selling to magazines is really an art and a science in itself. I love the writing field and continually try to improve my marketing techniques. I would appreciate hearing from you about how you were able to put this book to work. I would also like to know about any methods you might have developed that have resulted in increased sales. I look forward to hearing from you.

Duane Newcomb
% Writer's Digest Books
1507 Dana Avenue
Cincinnati, OH 45207

Appendix A

GOVERNMENT PHOTO COLLECTIONS

Agency for International
Development
Office of Public Affairs
Room 4886
Washington, DC 20523
(202)632-9309
Foreign aid project photos

Department of Agriculture
Photography Division
Office of Governmental and
Public Affairs Staff
South Building, Room 4407
Washington, DC 20250
(202)447-6633
Agriculture, forest, soil, and
home economics photos

Department of Commerce
Office of Publications
Fourteenth & E Streets, NW
Room 2830-B
Washington, DC 20230
(202)377-2021
Photos concerning the nation's
foreign and domestic commerce

Department of Defense
Audio-Visual Division
Office of the Assistant Secretary
of Defense/Public Affairs
The Pentagon, Room 2E773
Washington, DC 20301
(202)697-1252
Weapons and Equipment photos

Department of Housing and
Urban Development
Photography Lab
451 Seventh St., SW
Washington, DC 20410
Federally assisted housing project
photos

Department of State
Office of Visual Services
OPR/VS
Room B-258
Washington, DC 20520
(202)632-1634
Diplomatic functions photos

Department of Transportation
Publishing and Graphics Division
400 Seventh St., SW
Room 2317
Washington, DC 20590
(202)426-1015
Transportation photos

Environmental Protection Agency
Documeria
401 M St., SW
West Tower, Room 227
Washington, DC 20460
(202)755-0138
Environmental pictures

Export-Import Bank
Office of Public Affairs
811 Vermont Ave., NW
Washington, DC 20571
(202)566-8990
Pictures of foreign projects of the
bank

Food and Drug Administration
Office of Public Affairs
HFI-20
5600 Fishers Lane
Rockville, MD 20857
(301)443-3220
Food- and drug-related pictures

Library of Congress
Prints of Photographs Division
Washington, DC 20243
(202)287-6394
Millions of photographs on
many subjects

National Aeronautics and
Space Administration
Audio/Visuals
NASA Headquarters
400 Maryland Ave. SW
Room 6035
Washington, DC 20904
(202)755-8366
Photos of activities of the
space program

National Park Service
Department of the Interior
Photo Library
Eighteenth & E Streets, NW
8th Floor
Washington, DC 20240
(202)343-5055
National parks and
monuments photos

National Archives
Still Pictures Division
Seventh & Pennsylvania Ave.,
NW, 18th Floor
Washington, DC 20408
(202)523-3236
Millions of historical photographs

Appendix B

COMMERCIAL DATABASES

ADP Network Services, Inc.
175 Jackson Plaza
Ann Arbor, MI 48106
(313)769-6800

Bowne Information Systems
435 Hudson Street
New York, NY 10014
(212)807-7280

BRS (Bibliographic
Retrieval Services)
1200 Route 7
Latham, NY 12110
(800)833-4707

Chase Econometrics/Interactive
Data Corporation
150 Monument Road
Bala Cynwyd, PA 19004
(215)896-4772

CISI Network Corporation
PSC Division
16625 Saticoy Street
Van Nuys, CA 91406
(213)781-8221

CitiShare
P.O. Box 1127
New York, NY 10043
(212)559-0787

CompuServe, Inc.
5000 Arlington Center Blvd.
Columbus, OH 43220
(800)848-8900

Computer Sciences Corporation
Infonet Division
1616 N. Fort Myer Drive
Arlington, VA 22209
(703)841-3500

COMSHARE, Inc.
P.O. Box 1588
3001 S. State Street
Ann Arbor, MI 48106
(313)994-4800

Control Data Corporation
Business Information Services
500 W. Putnam Avenue
P.O. Box 7100
Greenwich, CT 06836
(202)622-2000

DIALOG Information
Services Inc.
3460 Hillview Avenue
Palo Alto, CA 94304
(800)227-1927

Dow Jones and Company, Inc.
P.O. Box 300
Princeton, NJ 08540
(800)257-5114

General Electric
Information Services
401 N. Washington Street
Rockville, MD 20850
(301)340-3536

GTE Information Services Inc.
East Park Drive
Mount Laurel, NJ 08054
(609)235-7300

Inforonics, Inc.
550 Newton Road
Littleton, MA 01460
(617)486-8976

Management Science
Associates, Inc.
5100 Centre Avenue
Pittsburgh, PA 15232
(412)398-9100

National Computer Network of
Chicago, Inc.
1929 N. Harlem Avenue
Chicago, IL 60635
(312)622-6666

National Library of Medicine
MEDLARS Management Section
8600 Rockville Pike
Bethesda, MD 20209
(301)496-6193

NewsNet, Inc.
945 Haverford Road
Bryn Mawr, PA 19010
(800)345-1301

On-Line Research, Inc.
151 Railroad Avenue
Greenwich, CT 06830

Rapidata Division
National Data Corporation
20 New Dutch Lane
Fairfield, NJ 07006
(201)227-0035

SDC Information Services
2500 Colorado Avenue
Santa Monica, CA 90406
(800)421-7229

Telstat Systems, Inc.
60 Hudson Street
New York, NY 10031
(212)227-5082

United Information Services, Inc.
P.O. Box 8551
Kansas City, MO 64114
(913)341-9161

Windsor Systems
Development Inc.
545 Fifth Avenue, Suite 909
New York, NY 10017
(212)697-5390

Select Bibliography

If I had to select one book to help me market my articles and books, it would be *Writer's Market*. As far as I'm concerned, this is the writer's bible. The other books listed here will make marketing what you write a much simpler task.

Bacons Publicity Checker. Chicago, Illinois: Bacons Publishing Co., annual. Lists newspapers, business publications, and magazines.

Barnhart, Helene Schellenberg. *How to Write and Sell the Eight Easiest Article Types.* Cincinnati, Ohio: Writer's Digest Books, 1985. Identifies the eight easiest-to-sell articles and gives step-by-step, how-to-sell information.

Brohaugh, William. *Professional Etiquette for Writers.* Cincinnati, Ohio: Writer's Digest Books, 1986. Explains how to deal with editors successfully.

Cool, Lisa Collier. *How to Sell Every Magazine Article You Write.* Cincinnati, Ohio: Writer's Digest Books, 1986. This excellent guide for selling your writing especially emphasizes the major magazines.

Cool, Lisa Collier. *How to Write Irresistible Query Letters.* Cincinnati, Ohio: Writer's Digest Books, 1987. Spells out the details of composing effective queries.

Editor and Publisher International Year Book. New York, New York: Editor and Publisher, annual. Lists American and foreign daily newspapers.

Encyclopedia of Associations. Detroit, Michigan: Gale Research, annual.

Europa Yearbook. London, England: Europa Publications, Ltd., annual. Lists magazine publishers worldwide. Can be ordered by writing the publisher at 18 Bedford Square, London WC1B-3JN, England.

Glossbrenner, Alfred. *How to Look It Up Online—Get the Information Edge with Your Personal Computer.* New York, New York: St. Martin's Press, 1987. Choosing and using the major online information services (databases).

Horowitz, Lois. *Knowing Where to Look: The Ultimate Guide to Research.* Cincinnati, Ohio: Writer's Digest Books, 1984. How to do the best research with the least wasted time and effort.

Horowitz, Lois. *A Writer's Guide to Research.* Cincinnati, Ohio: Writer's Digest Books, 1986. A streamlined guide for finding the facts you need.

Kevles, Barbara. *Basic Magazine Writing.* Cincinnati, Ohio: Writer's Digest Books, 1986. A good guide to the basic article forms.

Larsen, Michael. *How to Write a Book Proposal.* Cincinnati, Ohio: Writer's Digest Books, 1985. Although I wish Michael had kept his outlines much shorter and to the point, this is the best guide available for writing book proposals and outlines. No writer who expects to sell a book should be without it.

Lesko, Matthew. *The Computer Data and Database Sourcebook.* New York, New York: Avon Books, 1984. A complete encyclopedia of commercial and public sources of information for use with any computer.

Religious Writer's Marketplace. Philadelphia, Pennsylvania: Running Press, annual. A must if you are writing for the religious markets.

Scott, DeWitt. *How to Write.* Los Alamitos, California: Harmon Publishing, 1984. A small but useful book that will help anyone write simply and clearly.

Standard Rate and Data. Wilmette, Illinois: Standard Rate and Data Service, monthly. Separate volumes list business publications, consumer magazines, and newspapers.

Ulrich's International Periodicals Directory. New York: R.R. Bowker, biennial. An essential guide for any writer interested in the global market.

Working Press of the Nation. Vol. 5. Chicago, Illinois: National Research Bureau, annual. Covers company, organization, and group publications.

Writer's Handbook. Boston, Massachusetts: The Writer, Inc., annual. Contains about 2,000 market listings plus a number of useful articles on writing and marketing.

Writer's Market. Cincinnati, Ohio: Writer's Digest Books, annual. The best overall directory available. This directory lists between 4,000 and 5,000 markets for the freelance writer.

Zobell, Louise. *Travel Writer's Handbook.* Cincinnati, Ohio: Writer's Digest Books, 1984. Explains how to write and sell travel articles.

Index

OTHER BOOKS IN THE
WRITER'S BASIC BOOKSHELF
SERIES

A Beginner's Guide to Getting Published, edited by Kirk Polking, $10.95

How to Bulletproof Your Manuscript, by Bruce B. Henderson, $9.95

How to Sell & Re-Sell Your Writing, by Duane Newcomb, $11.95

How to Understand & Negotiate a Book Contract or Magazine Agreement, by Richard Balkin, $11.95

How to Write & Sell Column, by Julie Raskin & Carolyn Males, $10.95

How to Write a Book Proposal, by Michael Larsen, $9.95

Literary Agents: How to Get & Work with the Right One for You, by Michael Larsen, $9.95

Professional Etiquette for Writers, by William Brohaugh, $9.95

The 29 Most Common Writing Mistakes & How to Avoid Them, by Judy Delton, $9.95

A Writer's Guide to Research, by Lois Horowitz, $9.95

(For a complete catalog of Writer's Digest Books, write to the address below or call TOLL-FREE 1-800-543-4644, outside Ohio.)

To order directly from the publisher, include $2.00 postage and handling for one book, 50¢ for each additional book. Allow 30 days for delivery. Send to:

Writer's Digest Books
1507 Dana Avenue
Cincinnati, OH 45207

Prices subject to change without notice.